PENGUIN

POETIC

ARISTOTLE was born at Stageira, in the dominion of the kings of Macedonia, in 384 BC. For twenty years he studied at Athens in the Academy of Plato, on whose death in 347 he left, and, some time later, became tutor of the young Alexander the Great. When Alexander succeeded to the throne of Macedonia in 336, Aristotle returned to Athens and established his school and research institute, the Lyceum, to which his great erudition attracted a large number of scholars. After Alexander's death in 323, anti-Macedonian feeling drove Aristotle out of Athens, and he fled to Chalcis in Euboea, where he died in 322. His writings, which were of extraordinary range, profoundly affected the whole course of ancient and medieval philosophy, and they are still eagerly studied and debated by philosophers today. Very many of them have survived and among the most famous are the *Ethics* and the *Politics*, both of which are published in Penguin Classics, together with *The Athenian Constitution*, *De Anima*, *The Art of Rhetoric*, *Poetics* and the *Metaphysics*.

MALCOLM HEATH was born in London in 1957 and was educated in Harrow and at Oxford University. He was a lecturer in Greek for a year at the University of St Andrews, and then at the University of Leeds. Since 2000 he has been Professor of Greek Language and Literature at the University of Leeds. Apart from numerous articles, he has also published *The Poetics of Greek Tragedy* (1987), *Political Comedy in Aristophanes* (1987), *Unity in Greek Poetics* (1989) and *Hermogenes on Issues: Strategies of Argument in Later Greek Rhetoric* (1995).

# ARISTOTLE
## *Poetics*

*Translated with an introduction and notes by*
MALCOLM HEATH

PENGUIN BOOKS

PENGUIN BOOKS

Published by the Penguin Group
Penguin Books Ltd, 80 Strand, London WC2R 0RL, England
Penguin Putnam Inc., 375 Hudson Street, New York, New York 10014, USA
Penguin Books Australia Ltd, 250 Camberwell Road, Camberwell, Victoria 3124, Australia
Penguin Books Canada Ltd, 10 Alcorn Avenue, Toronto, Ontario, Canada M4V 3B2
Penguin Books India (P) Ltd, 11 Community Centre, Panchsheel Park, New Delhi – 110 017, India
Penguin Books (NZ) Ltd, Cnr Rosedale and Airborne Roads, Albany, Auckland, New Zealand
Penguin Books (South Africa) (Pty) Ltd, 24 Sturdee Avenue, Rosebank 2196, South Africa

Penguin Books Ltd, Registered Offices: 80 Strand, London WC2R 0RL, England

www.penguin.com

This edition first published 1996
9

Copyright © Malcolm Heath, 1996
All rights reserved

The moral right of the editor has been asserted

Filmset in 10/13pt Monotype Bembo
Typeset by Datix International Limited, Bungay, Suffolk
Printed in England by Clays Ltd, St Ives plc

# CONTENTS

INTRODUCTION     vii

  1. *Human culture, poetry and the* Poetics     ix

  2. *Imitation*     xii

  3. *Aristotle's history of poetry*     xv

  4. *The analysis of tragedy*     xviii

  5. *Plot: the basics*     xxii

  6. *Reversal and recognition*     xxviii

  7. *The best kinds of tragic plot*     xxxi

  8. *The pleasures of tragedy*     xxxv

  9. *The other parts of tragedy*     xliii

10. *Tragedy: miscellaneous aspects*     xlviii

11. *Epic*     liv

12. *Comedy*     lxii

13. *Further reading*     lxiv

14. *Reference conventions*     lxvi

NOTES TO THE INTRODUCTION     lxviii

SYNOPSIS OF THE *POETICS*     lxxii

POETICS     I

NOTES TO THE TRANSLATION     49

# INTRODUCTION

Aristotle was much admired in the ancient world for the elegance and clarity of his style. Unfortunately, the writings which earned him that esteem have not survived. What we read today are not the books which Aristotle prepared and polished for publication, but notes (perhaps in many cases lecture-notes) compiled for his own use or the use of his students. This has one great advantage: the Aristotelian works available to us, making no concessions to a lay readership, are the ones which intellectually sophisticated commentators in late antiquity found philosophically most rewarding. But there are also disadvantages. These texts were not designed for public consumption, and are consequently often very difficult to understand. The process by which they took their present form is unclear; in some cases there are signs of editorial activity (either by Aristotle himself or by a later hand); so different versions may have been spliced together, and what is presented as a single continuous text may in fact juxtapose different stages in the development of Aristotle's thinking. In general the style is cryptic, condensed and allusive; the *Poetics*, in particular, contains many passages which are more than usually obscure, as the notes to this translation will testify.

This situation has a paradoxical consequence. The works which did most to disseminate Aristotle's ideas on poetry in the ancient world were the three books *On Poets* (written, like Plato's works, in the form of a dialogue and presumably more lucid than the extant *Poetics*) and the six books of *Homeric Problems*, which discussed passages in Homer faulted by critics as implausible, inconsistent or morally improper. Except for scattered fragments quoted by other ancient authors these two works have been lost.[1] The *Poetics* itself does not seem to have been widely known in antiquity. By contrast, since the Renaissance its influence on literary theorists and critics has been massive; but the obscurities of the text have left it open to a wide range of conflicting interpretations. There have been, and still are, fundamental disagreements about the meaning even of key concepts, like *hamartia* and *katharsis*.

The historic influence of the *Poetics* is one reason why it merits continued attention. Much of Western thinking about poetry and drama from the sixteenth century onwards will be obscure to those who are unfamiliar with the text which lies behind it. It is of course possible to take an interest in the variety of meanings which this text has had for successive generations of later readers without concerning oneself with the meanings which Aristotle himself might have been seeking to convey. There are, however, various reasons why it may also be worth taking an interest in what Aristotle meant.

One reason is that it may help us to a better understanding of Greek tragedy. We have in the *Poetics* an analysis of tragedy by an intelligent and well-informed observer who was much closer, chronologically and culturally, to the plays than we are; it would be irresponsible for the student of Greek tragedy to ignore his testimony. To be sure, Aristotle was not a direct contemporary of the great fifth-century tragedians whose plays have survived;[2] and although he numbered later tragedians (such as Theodectes) among his acquaintances, tragedy in the fourth century was not the same as tragedy in the fifth – as Aristotle himself was aware. There is no reason to assume that Aristotle's understanding of tragedy was either faultless or uncontroversial. It is widely accepted that he failed to appreciate fully the significance of the gods in fifth-century tragedy; and it is clear from polemical remarks in the *Poetics* itself that his views on a number of issues diverged from those of some at least of his contemporaries. We must show due caution, then, in using the *Poetics* as an aid to understanding the nature of Greek tragedy. But that is true of any body of evidence, and is no reason to neglect it.

Another reason why the *Poetics* is worth studying closely is the quality of its thought. Aristotle had an exceptionally penetrating and subtle intellect. Concepts and arguments which at first seem impenetrable often prove to make illuminating sense when further reflection brings to light their underlying rationale. For me, the challenge of trying to understand Aristotle's thought is the main reason why the *Poetics* continues to be such a rewarding text to study. This desire to understand is something with which Aristotle himself would have been in sympathy; indeed, it provides us with an excellent starting-point in trying to place the *Poetics* in the broader context of his philosophical work.

## 1. *Human culture, poetry and the* Poetics

'All human beings by nature desire knowledge.' This, the opening sentence of the *Metaphysics* (980a1),[3] states a fundamental premise of Aristotle's understanding of what it is to be human. He points out as evidence for his claim the pleasure we take in looking at things and assimilating information through our senses. Sensation is of course shared with many other animals, and the accretion of sensation through memory into experience is shared with some. But humans are unique in their capacity to derive universal judgements from their experiences. Animals act by instinct or acquired habit, but humans are capable of acting from understanding: they know (as a dog might know) *that* this is the thing to do in a certain situation, but they may also understand (as a dog cannot) *why* it is the thing to do. This is what Aristotle calls in Greek *tekhnê*; the word is conventionally translated as 'craft', 'skill' or 'art', but Aristotle defines *tekhnê* as a productive capacity informed by an understanding of its intrinsic rationale (cf. *Nicomachean Ethics*, 1140a20f.). For Aristotle, the evolution of human culture is in large part the evolution of *tekhnê*. The first arts which human beings developed were those concerned with producing the necessities of their existence. Then came recreational arts – those which, while not necessary, enhance the quality of human life. In due course, activities arose which simply satisfy the desire to know (Aristotle's example is mathematics). Ultimately, philosophy emerged. Philosophy is rooted in the basic human instinct to seek knowledge: the world puzzles us and arouses our sense of wonder, and so prompts us to look for explanations. Philosophy is therefore the sophisticated descendant of primitive myth-making responses to an astonishing world.

Aristotle's sketch of human culture is relevant in a number of ways to the *Poetics*. Human beings produce, among other things, poems, and the production of poems too can be a *tekhnê*; it is an activity with its own intrinsic rationale, and it can be rendered intelligible. This does not mean that poets themselves necessarily understand what they are doing. In the *Poetics* Aristotle does not treat it as a matter of any consequence whether a given poet has a reflective understanding of his craft. In chapter 8 he leaves open the question of whether Homer's grasp of correct plot-structure was due to *tekhnê* or to instinct (51a24). In chapter 14 he suggests that early dramatists discovered the best stories to use in tragedy by chance rather than by *tekhnê* (54a9–12); trial and error established a repertoire of first-rate tragic stories, but the dramatists would not have been able to explain why those stories were best (as Aristotle thinks he can). In his discussion of *tekhnê* at the beginning of the *Metaphysics* Aristotle notes that unreflective experience may produce the same result as *tekhnê* (981a12–15). In general, the ability to do something well does not depend on understanding, nor does understanding necessarily imply an ability to do it well. A joiner taught to make a piece of furniture in a particular way may do it perfectly, even if he does not understand the reasons why that is the best way to do it; he may even do it better than a colleague who has more understanding but less manual dexterity.

There are reasons why this principle might apply to poetry especially. Poets must be able to project themselves into the emotions of others; natural talent, or even a touch of insanity, are necessary for this (55a30–4). Moreover, metaphor (which Aristotle regards as the most important feature of poetic language) depends on the ability to perceive similarities; this, he says, is a natural gift and cannot be taught (59a4–8). Aristotle is unlikely to have assumed, therefore, that reading the *Poetics* would make someone good at composing poetry, and it is unrealistic to think of the *Poetics* as a do-it-yourself manual for would-be poets. Aristotle's interest is philosophical; that is, it is driven by his desire to understand. The production of good poems is an activity that can be understood, and the *Poetics* is an attempt to lay that intelligibility open to inspection. It is no surprise that Aristotle thought this attempt worth making. His own appetite for understanding was omnivorous (he did pioneering work in – among other things – logic, physics and metaphysics, biology, psychology, ethics and politics), and poetry was an important feature in the public culture of ancient Greek communities. Indeed, poetry had always excited the wonder which Aristotle sees as the root of philosophical enquiry: the Greeks habitually talked of the intense pleasure to be derived from poetry, and of the bewitching enchantment it could work.

Aristotle may also have believed that understanding of the kind he pursues in the *Poetics* can enhance the pleasure which poetry gives us. A pointer to this can be found in one of his biological works, where he pre-empts objections to the trivial and unpleasant nature of some of the organisms he will be studying (*Parts of Animals*, 645a8–15):

There are animals which are unattractive to the senses when one studies them; but even in these, nature's craftsmanship provides innumerable pleasures for those who can discern the causes and have an aptitude for philosophy. It would be unreasonable – in fact, absurd – if we got pleasure from studying pictures of these things, because then we are at the same time studying the art [*tekhnê*] which crafted them (e.g. the art of painting or sculpture), but did not get even more pleasure from studying the actual products of nature – at least when we can make out their causes.

Understanding why an insect or a worm has the form it does is a source of pleasure; this is analogous to the pleasure which can be

derived from the study of a painting if one has an understanding
of its *tekhnê* – that is, of the reasons why this was the right way to
depict that subject. The analogy implies a sophisticated observer. We
have seen that Aristotle leaves it an open question whether poets
proceed by *tekhnê*, by instinct or by trial and error, and the same can
be assumed for painters. We cannot suppose that any casual observer
will have a more explicit grasp of the requirements of *tekhnê* than
the artist; so Aristotle must be comparing the expert naturalist's
pleasure in the understanding of natural phenomena to the pleasure
which an expert critic derives from his or her appreciation of a
painter's skill. As we shall see, Aristotle regards poetry and painting
as fundamentally similar activities; so the *Poetics* may enhance the
pleasure we derive from a well-constructed play by helping us to
understand why it is good.

## 2. *Imitation*

The passage from *Parts of Animals* explains a pleasure which expert
critics can derive from the skilful depiction even of unprepossessing
objects. The expertise on which this pleasure depends is not to be
expected of the majority of people who view such paintings; but
everyone can gain pleasure from them. A more general explanation
for this phenomenon is needed, therefore, and Aristotle provides it
in chapter 4 of the *Poetics*. Here he roots the visual arts in the human
desire for knowledge (48b10–19, cf. *Rhetoric*, 1371b4–10). Someone
looking at a painting needs to recognize it as a depiction of a given
object (as a portrait of, for example, Socrates). This act of recognition
involves an exercise of our capacity for cognition; and the exercise of
any capacity is, for Aristotle, in itself pleasurable (*Nicomachean Ethics*,
1174b14–5a21).

This passage in chapter 4 of the *Poetics* is one of many in which
Aristotle refers to painting and the visual arts in order to make a
point about poetry. He regards these analogies as valid because he

believes both painting and poetry to be forms of *mimêsis*, a word
which I shall translate as 'imitation'.[4] Many scholars would object to
this rendering, and prefer 'representation'. All translations are, of
course, to some extent inadequate, and 'imitation' is by no means
perfect; but there are two reasons why 'representation' may be particularly unhelpful in this context. First, it fails to capture an essential
element in Aristotle's concept of *mimêsis* – that of a similarity which
does not rest wholly on convention. For example, an arbitrary
symbol on a map may 'represent' an airport, but the representation is
purely conventional; the symbol is not a *mimêsis* of the airport. A
scaled outline of its runways would be a *mimêsis*. Aristotle is quite
explicit in linking *mimêsis* and similarity even in cases where we
would find it odd to speak of 'imitation'; he says, for example, that
melody and rhythm can be 'likenesses' and 'imitations' of character
and emotion (*Politics*, 1340a18–23, 38f.), effectively equating the two
terms. Secondly, 'representation' fails to capture the full range of
Aristotle's concept. The use of a quasi-technical term of modern
aesthetics may tend to obscure the continuity which Aristotle per-
ceives between *mimêsis* in painting, poetry and music and in other,
non-artistic forms of activity, such as the mimicry of animal noises
and other sounds (*Poetics*, 47a20, cf. Plato, *Republic*, 397a, *Laws*, 669c–
d) and children's play-acting (*Poetics*, 48b7f., cf. *Politics*, 1336a32–4).
This continuity is essential to Aristotle's argument in chapter 4 of
the *Poetics*; his point there is precisely that poetry is an expression of
a human instinct for *mimêsis* that is also displayed in more elementary forms of behaviour.

Aristotle's contention, then, is that human beings are by nature
prone to engage in the creation of likenesses, and to respond to
likenesses with pleasure, and he explains this instinct by reference
to their innate desire for knowledge. A likeness is (by definition) a
likeness *of* something; to take part in the activity of making and responding to likenesses we must recognize the relationship between
the likeness and its object. This engages and satisfies the desire to
exercise our distinctively human power of understanding, and is

therefore pleasurable. This exercise of our capacity for understanding is, to be sure, a rudimentary one. But Aristotle's purpose here is to explain how poetry and painting are rooted in basic instincts shared by even the least intellectually sophisticated people. When Aristotle discerns the roots of philosophy in a primitive sense of wonder there is no implication that philosophy has been explained away or cheapened. Likewise, the contention that poetry is ultimately explicable as an expression of the elementary human desire for knowledge does not, and is not meant to, provide an exhaustive account of poetry. Indeed, Aristotle goes on in the rest of chapter 4 to trace the development of poetry from primitive improvisation to increasingly complex and sophisticated forms. We shall see in due course that the *Poetics* implies a correspondingly complex analysis of what poetry has to offer its audiences (§8).

The notion of poetry as imitation raises many complex problems which cannot be explored in depth here.[5] But some points must be stressed. An imitation need not be a straightforward copy of the object imitated; the similarity between the object and its likeness may reside in a more oblique and abstract correspondence (as the doctrine that music contains 'likenesses' of states of character proves). Nor need an imitation be a likeness of an object which actually exists. It is clear from chapter 9 that Aristotle is indifferent to whether the events recounted in a poem did or did not happen in reality; historiographical texts are judged by the criterion of fidelity to real events, but poems are not. Aristotle's concept of poetry as imitation is therefore consistent with (although not identical to) that of fiction. Indeed, the events in a poem do not even have to conform to the basic structure of reality. Aristotle's dictum that poetry is concerned, not with what *has* happened, but with 'the kind of thing that *would* happen, i.e. what is possible in accordance with probability or necessity' (51a36–8) must be read in the light of the application of his critical principles in chapter 25. For example, Aristotle did not believe that the theology built into traditional Greek myths was true; but (unlike some earlier philosophers, including Plato) he had no objection to poetic plots based on them (60b35–61a1). A poem which recounts the actions of a vengeful deity is not an imitation of something which (in Aristotle's view) does or could exist in the real world; but it is an imitation of the kind of thing which would necessarily or probably happen if the traditional beliefs about the gods were true.

### 3. Aristotle's history of poetry

Having established poetry's ultimate anthropological roots at the beginning of chapter 4, Aristotle goes on to sketch the process by which more sophisticated forms of poetry evolved. The theoretical framework for this outline history of poetry is provided by the first three chapters, which construct a matrix of three different ways in which poems can be distinguished from other kinds of imitation and from each other – in terms of their medium, object and mode.

First, why *poetry*? The pleasure which human beings by nature derive from imitations in general does not explain why they took up this form of imitation in particular. According to chapter 1, poetry is differentiated from other kinds of imitation by the medium in which it produces its likenesses: poetry is imitation in rhythmical language, with or without melodic accompaniment. It is important to note that the weight of emphasis in Aristotle's analysis falls on the element of imitation.[6] His contemporaries would have been content to define poetry as composition in verse; by contrast, Aristotle denies that non-imitative forms of verse are poetry. In saying this he is not making an aesthetic judgement. As an example of someone who composes verse but is not a poet Aristotle cites the philosopher Empedocles; but we know that he had a high regard for the artistic qualities of Empedocles' verse. Aristotle is not distinguishing poetry from other forms of verse in terms of its linguistic artistry; he is concerned solely with the use to which the verse is put – is it imitation or not? Nevertheless, verse is a traditional medium for imitation, and this fact needs to be explained. Aristotle believes that human beings have an instinct for rhythm and melody, as they do for imitation. This claim, made in passing in chapter 4 (48b20f.), is echoed later when rhythm and song are identified as features which make the language of tragedy pleasurable (49b28f.). The pleasure which human beings take in rhythm and melody makes it natural that their instinct for imitation should be expressed in the medium of verse and song.

Aristotle conjectures, not unreasonably, that imitation in verse and song would have begun with simple improvisations, out of which the highly sophisticated forms of poetry known in his own day would gradually have developed. Aristotle's account of this development is sometimes criticized for imposing models of growth derived from his biological research. This is misleading. In one sense, the evolution of poetic forms *is* a natural process. If, as Aristotle believes, poetry expresses a number of human instincts (such as those for imitation, rhythm and melody), it is an activity in which human beings will by nature tend to engage. Moreover, poets are likely over time to discover better and better ways of doing it, if only by experiment; thus tragic poets (in Aristotle's view) found the best kind of tragic plot by trial and error (54a9–12). Once the optimum form of anything has been achieved, further development of it is by definition impossible; thereafter, there can only be (at best) a proliferation of different instances of that optimum form. It is in this sense that Aristotle can say that 'after undergoing many transformations tragedy came to rest, because it had attained its natural state' (49a14f.). But in chapters 4 and 5 he displays considerable interest in individual contributions to the development of poetry, and he is aware that social and institutional factors, as well as individual incompetence, may inhibit the continued realization of the optimum form (51b35–52a1, 53a33–5). Clearly, then, Aristotle saw the history of poetry as a social, and not simply as a natural, phenomenon.[7]

The assumed trajectory of development will depend on what kind of poetry one regards as most sophisticated. Aristotle works from two premises. The first is that poetry is better if it has a structured plot. He infers that the earliest poems would have recounted the glorious deeds of some god or hero admiringly, or the wicked or inept deeds of some inferior character in a satirical vein, without there being any structured sequence to the events described. In due course, these disjointed strings of admirable or contemptible actions gave way to connected narratives, as in epic. The importance of a coherently structured plot is a crucial element in the *Poetics*, and we shall examine its implications in detail later (§5–7).

Aristotle's second premise is that poetry is better if (to use the terminology of chapter 3) its mode is dramatic rather than narrative. Poetry is imitation; it seeks to create likenesses, and the likeness is greater if the words of those involved in the action are presented directly rather than being mediated by a narrator. Hence Aristotle's admiring remarks on Homer in chapter 24 (60a5–9):

Homer deserves praise for many reasons, but above all because he alone among poets is not ignorant of what he should do in his own person. The poet in person should say as little as possible; that is not what makes him an imitator. Other poets perform in person throughout, and imitate little and seldom.

The implication that epic narrative as such is not imitation seems at first sight to contradict what is said of it elsewhere in the *Poetics*, but the paradox is only superficial. The purest form of poetic imitation is in the dramatic mode; other modes are imitative, but not in the same degree.[8] The Homeric poems, with their high proportion of direct speech, therefore represent the highest possible development of epic, but also disclose a potential which cannot be fully realized within the constraints of narrative form. So Homer points the way towards drama; but drama proper was (in Aristotle's view) a separate and subsequent development. His hypothesis is that it originated as an adaptation of improvisatory poetic forms in which a soloist led and responded to a chorus (49a9–14); the distinction between chorus and chorus-leader opens up the possibility of dialogue, and hence of drama. The leader thus became the first actor; as poets perceived and increasingly exploited the dramatic possibilities of spoken dialogue the number of actors was increased to three, and the chorus declined in importance (49a15–19) – indeed, by Aristotle's day its importance had declined more than he thought appropriate (56a25–32).

So Aristotle sees the history of poetry as a development towards greater coherence in plot-structure, and towards the more truly imitative dramatic mode. But the dichotomy between the imitation of admirable and inferior agents and activities which he assumes was present in the earliest poetry remains constant. Chapter 2 explained its theoretical rationale, and it can be observed to persist throughout the history of poetry: praise-poems are balanced by lampoons, heroic epic by narrative burlesques, tragedy by comedy. The *Poetics* concentrates on tragedy, the most highly developed form of poetry concerned with superior persons. Epic is given relatively brief treatment as a pendant to tragedy. A full discussion of comedy is promised (49b21f.), but the promise is not fulfilled in the extant *Poetics*; this is one of several indications that the text we have is incomplete.

## 4. *The analysis of tragedy*

The framework for the analysis of tragedy is set out in chapter 6. A famous definition states what tragedy is; from this Aristotle deduces the constituent parts of tragedy; he then ranks these constituents in order of importance, giving primacy to plot.

Tragedy, like all poetry, is an imitation. Specifically, it is an imitation of a certain kind of action. So one constituent part of tragedy is *plot*, the ordered sequence of events which make up the action being imitated. An action is performed by agents, and agents necessarily have moral and intellectual characteristics, expressed in what they do and say. From this we can deduce that *character* and *reasoning* will also be constituent parts of tragedy. To see what Aristotle means by these two terms, imagine that you have left me alone with your silver spoons. Broadly speaking, there are two factors that will determine whether or not I steal them. One is whether I am honest; this is the kind of thing which Aristotle means by character – an agent's settled moral disposition. The other relevant factor is how I interpret the situation: do I think that I am likely to avoid suspicion if I take the spoons? This is what Aristotle means by reasoning. If I am dishonest and reason that I can get away with it, I am likely to steal the spoons; to use a phrase that recurs persistently throughout the *Poetics*, it is 'necessary or probable' that I will steal the spoons if I am dishonest and think I can get away with it. Thus character sets my agenda (what would I like to do?), and reasoning relates that agenda to a given situation (what is it feasible to do in these circumstances?).

Plot, character and reasoning relate to the object of tragic imitation. The medium of tragedy is rhythmical language, sometimes on its own and sometimes combined with melody. This gives us two further constituents of tragedy: *diction* and *lyric poetry*, respectively the spoken and the sung parts of the play's verbal text.

Tragedy is poetic imitation in the dramatic mode. It is designed to be acted out on-stage, where the action (unlike the action of an epic) can be seen. So tragedy also includes *spectacle* (the translation is conventional and unsatisfactory: it refers to everything that is visible on stage, and is not limited simply to striking effects). We must be cautious here. A tragedy is a poem, not a performance. A tragedy which, for whatever reason, is never performed is no less a tragedy; and a tragedy may be good, even if its performance is botched. So what is actually seen by a given audience on a given occasion is incidental to the play as such. Spectacle is a part of tragedy in the sense that tragedy (unlike epic) is potentially performable; so the poet has a duty to ensure that his text can be performed without visual absurdity (at 55a22–9 Aristotle cryptically mentions one poet's failure to achieve this). However, the actual realization of his text in visible stage-action is not the poet's responsibility, but that of the stage-manager and director. It is therefore not surprising that (at the end of chapter 6) Aristotle rates spectacle as the least important of tragedy's constituents.

More striking, perhaps, is the relatively low priority he gives to the verbal text of tragedy.[9] If poetry were defined as composition in verse, this down-rating of the linguistic text would be impossible to defend; but Aristotle has firmly rejected that definition in chapter 1, and from his perspective the low priority attached to language makes sense. Rhythmical language is tragedy's medium; it is a means to tragedy's end, that end being the imitation of an action. From this it is a reasonable inference that the choice of the action to be imitated is more crucial to achieving tragedy's effect than the way in which the imitation is realized in words. This is not to deny that an incompetent composer of verse could ruin a well-chosen tragic plot, nor that the deficiencies of a second-rate plot could be hidden by inspired verse. But the language is there to help realize the plot's potential, and in that sense is subordinate and secondary.

Aristotle's arguments for the primacy of plot are therefore primarily arguments for the primacy of plot over character. He begins by claiming that 'tragedy is not an imitation of persons, but of actions and of life' (50a16f.). The reason he gives is that good and bad fortune ('well-being and ill-being', as Aristotle puts it, highlighting the contrast in the Greek by an unusual choice of word for misfortune) depend on action. An outstandingly talented person is not necessarily outstandingly successful; talents have to be *exercised*. As Aristotle observes, in an athletic competition the prize is not awarded to the athlete in best condition, but to the one who actually comes first (*Eudemian Ethics*, 1219b9f., cf. *Nicomachean Ethics*, 1099a3–5). We can speak of success and failure, therefore, only in relation to the exercise of someone's abilities; and the outcome of this exercise will not be determined by the person's abilities alone, but is also influenced by the opportunities they have, and so forth. In this sense, therefore, it is action and not only character that determines success or failure. It should be noted that the Greek word *praxis* has a wider range of meanings than its conventional English translation, 'action'. If, using the corresponding verb, I ask someone '*Ti pratteis?*' I might be saying either 'What are you doing?' or 'How are you?' So *praxis* means 'action' not just in the sense of what someone *does* but also in the sense of how they *fare*. Aristotle will say in chapter 11 that suffering (*pathos*) is 'an action [*praxis*] that involves destruction or pain' (52b11f.); the apparent paradox in describing suffering as an action disappears when one takes account of the broad sense of *praxis*.

Success and failure depend on action, therefore. But why does Aristotle refer to success or failure? According to his definition, tragedy 'effect[s] through pity and fear the purification of such emotions' (49b27f.). We shall return in §8 to the difficult problem posed by 'purification' (*katharsis*); here it is sufficient to note that tragedy aims to excite a response of pity and fear. Tragedy is 'an imitation . . . of events that evoke fear and pity' (52a2f.). These emotions (which Aristotle analyses in detail in Book 2 of the *Rhetoric*, chapters 5 and 8) are responses to success and failure; for example, we pity the talented person who is prevented by adverse circumstance from achieving the success he or she deserves. (Note that in Aristotle's view we do not pity someone for a lack of talent; it is the lack of success which we pity, and our pity is greater when it is a talented person who fails than when the failure is in keeping with a person's ability.) So Aristotle's first argument for the primacy of plot is as follows: tragedy aims to excite fear and pity; these emotions are responses to success and failure; success and failure depend on action; hence action is the most essential thing in tragedy; therefore plot is the most important element.

The second argument approaches from the opposite direction: tragedy is impossible without plot, but it is possible without character; if character is dispensable, it cannot be as important as plot. The idea of drama without the depiction of character may seem surprising. In the context of the dichotomy of character and reasoning, the implication is a play in which action arises out of people's perception of and reasoning about the possibilities of a situation without any impression being conveyed of their underlying moral disposition. Knowledge of an individual's character is not essential to an understanding of their actions; we can hear reports of things done by complete strangers and recognize that their actions make sense in human terms, or be perplexed because they apparently do not. So in a tragedy without character motivation would be handled impersonally (this is what *someone* would do in this situation) rather than concretely (this is what a person with this particular set of characteristics would do). Aristotle does not suggest that such a tragedy would be as good as a tragedy with character; in fact, we know from the discussion of Homer's treatment of character that he would not (60a10f.). His point is only that if such a tragedy is possible in principle, then character cannot be essential to tragedy in the way that plot is.

## 5. *Plot: the basics*

Aristotle's emphasis on the primacy of plot is reflected in the amount of space he allocates to it: chapters 7–14 are devoted almost entirely to an analysis of plot. There are three stages in this analysis. Chapters 7–9 specify the minimum conditions which *any* plot must satisfy if it is to be well-formed. The end of chapter 9 and the next two chapters distinguish two kinds of plot, simple and complex; since Aristotle will claim that complex plots (in the technical sense he has defined) are superior to simple ones, this part of the discussion moves beyond the minimum conditions required of any plot and begins to consider what makes one well-formed plot *better* than another. This question is tackled more systematically in chapters 13–14, which address the question of the *best* kind of tragic plot.[10]

The definition at the beginning of chapter 6 stated that tragedy is an imitation of an action that is complete and has magnitude. These two concepts are taken up in chapter 7. The exposition of the con-

cept of *completeness* or wholeness (the terms are effectively equivalent)
introduces a famous dictum: 'A *whole* is that which has a beginning,
a middle and an end' (50b26f.). This is not (despite appearances) a
trivial observation. To call something a beginning, a middle or an
end in Aristotle's sense is not simply to comment on the position in
a series which it happens to have; the positions described are not
random, but necessary. Aristotle is talking about an *ordered structure*.
His definitions of beginning, middle and end show that there are
two aspects of the structure of a plot which he wants to bring out
when he uses these terms. First, the plot consists of a *connected* series
of events: one thing follows on another as a necessary consequence.
Secondly, the plot consists of a *self-contained* series of events: the first
thing in the series is in some sense self-explanatory – it is not a
necessary consequence of something else; equally, the last event in
the series brings it to a definite end – there is no further necessary
consequence in the series. Another term for this self-containment is
*closure*. The series of events which constitutes a well-formed plot is
therefore closed at both ends, and connected in between.

Consider by way of illustration a simple story: 'Bill strangled a cat.
Ben strangled a cat.' This is not a 'complete' plot in Aristotelian
terms. The two events have no necessary connection. So let us try
again: 'Bill strangled Ben's cat. So Ben strangled Bill's cat in retaliation.' This is better: we can now see how the two events hang together; the series of events is connected. But is it self-contained?
Why did the cat-strangling start in the first place? And was that the
end of it? Let us try once more: 'Bill thought that his cat was going
to lose to Ben's in the cat-show. So he strangled Ben's cat. Ben
strangled Bill's cat in retaliation. They never spoke to each other
again.' Now the story, connected and self-contained as it is, does satisfy Aristotle's criteria for being whole or complete. It has few other
virtues, but at this stage we are talking about the *minimum* criteria for
being a well-formed plot; we are not concerned with the qualities
which make one plot better than another.

Aristotle is often quoted as if he had said that a *play* has a beginning, a middle and an end. This is wrong. It is the *plot*, the underlying sequence of actions, that has this structure. To illustrate the distinction, consider Harold Pinter's *Betrayal*. This play traces the breakdown of a relationship in reverse chronological order: the opening scene shows the end of the process, and the scenes progress backward in time to its beginning. So the plot (the events which in Aristotle's terms are the object being imitated) runs in the opposite direction to the play which imitates it; the beginning of the one is the end of the other, and *vice versa*. To take a classical example, in the *Odyssey* the wanderings of Odysseus are included within the story of his home-coming by way of a retrospective narrative placed in the mouth of Odysseus himself. If the wanderings are counted as part of the plot, then the order of events in text and plot is different; if they are not counted as part of the plot (as the synopsis at 55b16–23 may imply), then part of the text is devoted to something other than an exposition of the plot. In either case, text and plot are distinct. Plot is therefore not co-extensive with the play; this is why Aristotle can refer to parts of the plot which fall outside the play (53b31f., 54b2–8, 55b24f., 60a27–32). The reader should be careful not to forget the level of abstraction at which Aristotle is working throughout the chapters on plot: he is not concerned here with the construction of the verbal artefacts which are tragedies, but with the design of the patterns of events which underlie them.

After defining completeness, Aristotle moves on to *magnitude*. In one sense it is trivial to say that a tragic plot must have magnitude: a plot of zero extent would not be a plot at all, since it would contain no events. The real question Aristotle wants to raise is more interesting: what is the *correct* magnitude of a tragic plot? In practice, the time available for a performance is a key determining factor, but this is a contingent fact about the organization of a particular theatrical event, and throws no light on the art of poetry as such. In principle, the upper limit is determined by what an audience can grasp at one time: it has to be possible for them to remember what is in the plot. The lower limit is determined by the need for the plot to include a change from bad fortune to good fortune, or from good to bad. The plot must have sufficient scope for such a change to take place. Moreover, it must take place in the way prescribed in the discussion of completeness. It is not enough to juxtapose prosperity and misery; the change from one to another must be the result of a sequence of necessarily connected events. If a successful cat-breeder wins a glittering prize and promptly commits suicide, the plot must show why he did so – out of remorse (as it may be) for having strangled his rival's cat.

The change of fortune is a new element, but fits in with Aristotle's first argument for the primacy of plot. The change from good fortune to bad corresponds to the failure in action that evokes pity. Unless the plot of tragedy has sufficient scope to allow for such a change, the emotional effect at which tragedy aims cannot be achieved. We must note, however, that Aristotle envisages the changes of fortune going in either direction; a change from bad fortune to good is also mentioned as a possibility. This may seem surprising: what has a change to good fortune to do with fear and pity? This is a question to which we shall return when we come to the discussion of the best kind (or kinds) of tragic plot in chapters 13 and 14.

When Aristotle discussed wholeness at the beginning of chapter 7 he talked about things following one on another in a necessary sequence. By the end of chapter 7 this requirement has been modified; here we find 'a series of events occurring sequentially in accordance with probability or necessity' (51a12f.); the pairing of necessity with probability will recur throughout the *Poetics*. In other works Aristotle explains these terms as referring to what happens always or usually; even in the early part of chapter 7 he was willing to speak about things following 'necessarily or in general' (50b30). It is necessary that the sun will rise tomorrow morning; the sun always rises in the morning. It is probable that I will get out of bed tomorrow morning; in general I do get up in the morning, but I might stay in bed all day if I am ill or have died or am feeling exceptionally idle.

Events in the human sphere are generally no more than probable; so this qualification of the initial formula makes it a little more realistic.

Chapter 8 introduces the concept of *unity*. Any imitation is unified if it imitates a single thing; so an imitation of an action will be unified if it imitates a single action (51a30–32).[11] By what criterion, then, are we to judge the singleness of an action? It cannot mean a single event; if a tragic plot involves a change of fortune, the single action will inevitably include a series of events. The analysis of completeness tells us that it must be a self-contained series of connected events, and Aristotle's criterion of unity does not add anything in substance to this analysis (nor should we expect it to: something complete and whole *is* a unity). But it allows him to formulate a negative point more sharply: the fact that a plot is concerned with the actions and experiences of a single person is not enough to make it unified, since there may be no necessary or probable connection between them. Consider another simple story: 'Bill got a statement from the bank; the next day he strangled Ben's cat.' This is not a unified plot by Aristotelian criteria; even though Bill is involved in both the incidents reported, there does not seem to be any necessary or probable connection between them.[12]

At the beginning of chapter 9 Aristotle takes a further step: 'It is also clear from what has been said that the function of the poet is not to say what *has* happened, but to say the kind of thing that *would* happen, i.e. what is possible in accordance with probability or necessity' (51a36–8). The distinction between what did happen and what would happen is not as sharp as it might seem at first glance; later in the chapter Aristotle observes that 'there is nothing to prevent some of the things which have happened from being the kind of thing which probably would happen' (51b30f.). The two classes therefore overlap; the poet can say what did happen, but only if it is also the kind of thing that would happen. In what cases, then, can something happen without being the kind of thing that would happen? Consider our last example. Even if this sequence of events actually happened, the lack of a necessary or probable connection means that it is not the kind of thing that would happen. If I tell you that Bill got another bank statement today, you will not jump to the conclusion that he is going to strangle another of Ben's cats tomorrow. In other words, when Aristotle speaks of 'the kind of thing that would happen', he is not talking about individual events but about connected sequences of events. If a poet wants to construct a plot out of a given sequence of events, it is not enough that those events actually happened; what is essential is that they are connected with each other in the way defined in chapter 7; and if they are so connected, it does not matter whether they actually happened or not.

Another way of putting this, which Aristotle discusses in chapter 9, is to say that poetry 'tends to express universals' (51b6f.). We must be careful here. Poetic plots do not deal in generalizations ('people usually get up in the morning'); they make statements about what a particular individual does at a particular time ('Bill got up this morning'). Indeed, the actions with which tragic plots are concerned are typically so exceptional that it would be absurd to talk of generalization. Orestes killed his mother; but it is not true that people generally kill their mothers, nor even that people like Orestes generally kill their mothers in such circumstances; such circumstances do not arise in general – that is one reason why Orestes' situation is such a potent basis for tragedy. But if the plot of Aeschylus' *Oresteia* is well-formed, then it is true that a person like Orestes would necessarily or probably kill his mother in such circumstances. So behind the particular statement about what Orestes did lies a premise about what such a person would necessarily or probably do in such circumstances; and this premise is a universal truth, however exceptional such persons and such circumstances may be in actuality. Poetry is concerned with particular sequences of events; but the connection between those events means that they instantiate universal structures.

To talk about universal structures is to talk about the things in which philosophy is interested. The universality of poetry therefore gives it something in common with philosophy. This is not to say that poetry is philosophy carried on by other means. Philosophy is *directly* concerned with universal truths, but poetry's concern is *indirect*: the universality of poetry is a by-product of its aim to construct effective plots. Consequently, while philosophy is concerned with universal *truths*, what lies behind an effective poetic plot may be the universalization of a conventional falsehood; hence, as we have seen (§2), Aristotle has no objections to plots based on traditional beliefs about the gods, even though he would dismiss those beliefs on philosophical grounds.

Historiography, by contrast, although bound to the truth of what happened, has no commitment to universality; history records what happened within a given period of time irrespective of whether the events form a sequence linked by necessity or probability.[13] Aristotle explicitly rejects plots constructed like works of historiography in chapter 23, just as he had rejected plots constructed like biographies in chapter 8 – a conclusion anticipated in his argument for the primacy of plot on the grounds that the emotions which tragedy aims to evoke are responses to success and failure: hence 'tragedy is not an imitation of persons, but of actions' (50a16f.).

## 6. *Reversal and recognition*

The end of chapter 9 introduces astonishment (*to thaumaston* in Greek covers a range of related ideas: surprise, amazement, wonder) into the discussion. Astonishment is a good thing in a tragic plot, but it is not a necessary thing in the way that wholeness and unity are. So here Aristotle moves on from the minimum conditions for a well-formed plot, and begins to consider what makes one such plot better than another. He refers at once to pity and fear: tragedy is an 'imitation not just of a complete action, but also of events that evoke fear and pity' (52a1–3). In judging the quality of one tragic plot over against another, it is their emotional impact to which Aristotle appeals. He identifies two things which make a sequence of events particularly effective: 'these effects occur above all when things come about contrary to expectation but because of one another' (52a3f.). 'Contrary to expectation' introduces the notion of astonishment, while 'because of one another' provides an anchor to the discussion of necessary or probable connection that has gone before. Astonishment and connection are both desirable if the emotional impact of the plot is to be maximized.

If connection is one of the things which increase emotional impact, we can see why Aristotle's theory of poetic plots places so much emphasis on it. But his slightly convoluted illustration of the importance of connection also suggests a degree of flexibility in practice. A man called Mitys is murdered; later, a statue of Mitys topples and kills his murderer. There is in fact no causal connection here, but it looks as if there was or ought to be such a connection; the two events seem to hang together, as if fate were bringing the murderer to justice or Mitys' vengeance were reaching out beyond the grave. Aristotle's argument is that the illusion of a connection increases our sense of astonishment at this series of events; if an illusion has that effect, then surely an actual connection must do so as well. There is ample evidence later in the *Poetics* of Aristotle's flexibility in this regard. In chapters 24 and 25 he approaches 'irrationalities' in the plot with caution, but does not absolutely rule them out. Aristotle sets out his requirements for a well-formed plot as things which in principle poetry ought to aim for, but his application of this principle is by no means rigid or doctrinaire; as we shall see (§11), he recognizes that departures from the norm he has defined may be advantageous in some circumstances.

Astonishment is not explicitly mentioned in chapters 10 and 11, but it is a crucial concept underlying the distinctions and definitions which they contain. Chapter 10 defines two classes of plot. A *simple* plot satisfies three conditions: the events are 'in the sense defined continuous and unified' (that is, connected in accordance with necessity or probability); there is a change of fortune (as specified in chapter 7); and there is no reversal or recognition. A *complex* plot also satisfies the first two conditions, but unlike the simple plot it does have reversal or recognition. These two terms are themselves defined in chapter 11.

Recognition (*anagnôrisis*) is 'a change from ignorance to knowledge' (52a29–31). The point is that this change affects the good or bad fortune of the person involved: Oedipus learns that he has killed his father and married his mother, and this recognition is the final blow that shatters his world. Note that recognition is associated above all with 'close relationship and enmity', on the grounds that such relationships have the closest bearing on an individual's good and bad fortune: Oedipus' world would not have been shattered if the man he had killed had turned out to be a complete stranger. This premise will be examined more closely in chapter 14 (see §7).

Reversal (*peripeteia*) is less straightforward. It is emphatically *not* to be equated with the tragic change of fortune: a change of fortune is a characteristic of all tragic plots, simple as well as complex, while reversal is distinctive to complex plots. But Aristotle's definition is vague: 'there is a change to the opposite in the actions being performed, as stated' (52a22f.). 'As stated' must refer to the discussion of astonishment; reversal involves an astonishing inversion of the expected outcome of some action, but that astonishment should not be achieved at the cost of necessary or probable connection. So, for example, Oedipus' discovery of the terrible truth is the paradoxical but necessary consequence of the arrival of a messenger who aims to bring good news and does everything he can to put an end to Oedipus' worries; here reversal and recognition reinforce each other (52a32f.).

The astonishment produced by reversal involves an overturn of expectation. There is therefore a close parallel between reversal and recognition: both reveal that the situation in which a character has been acting was misinterpreted. Reversal reveals that, because things are not what they seemed, the outcome of a person's actions will be other than what had been expected – for example, that the recipient of a message will be devastated rather than reassured. Recognition reveals that, because things are not what they seemed, what a person has done or is about to do is not what he thought it was – for example, that he has not killed a hostile stranger, as he supposed, but his own father. This parallel between reversal and recognition points the way to tragic error in chapter 13, and to the role of ignorance in chapter 14.

## 7. *The best kinds of tragic plot*

Chapters 13 and 14 address the question of the best kind of tragic plot. Both chapters assume that this is the plot that is most effective in arousing pity and fear, but they take different lines of approach and reach seemingly incompatible conclusions.

The approach in chapter 13 is to analyse in detail the tragic change of fortune. Aristotle identifies two variables in this change, which between them determine our emotional response to it: one is the direction of change (from good fortune to bad, or from bad to good); the other is the moral status of the person or persons involved in the change (virtuous or wicked). Since pity and fear are responses to bad fortune, the change from good fortune to bad is rated more highly than the reverse. But the fall of an outstandingly virtuous character into misfortune is morally repellent and disgusts us, while the fall of a bad character into misfortune is morally satisfying and pleases us; in both cases the response of pity is blocked by a contrary reaction. So the ideal tragic plot cannot be constructed around an exceptionally virtuous person or a wicked person; it must therefore be based on someone between these two – broadly speaking virtuous, but not outstandingly so. Because their virtue is not outstanding, we do not find their downfall morally repellent; because their downfall is undeserved, we can pity them.

If a tragic character does not fall into misfortune because he or she deserves to, what is the reason for the change in their fortune? Aristotle's answer introduces one of the most famous, and most often misunderstood, concepts of the *Poetics*: error. The Greek word *hamartia* covers making a mistake or getting something wrong in the most general sense; so the word itself gives little help in interpreting Aristotle's precise meaning, and we must be guided by the context. This at once excludes the interpretation of *hamartia* as a moral flaw: the second time Aristotle uses the word he speaks of a 'serious' *hamartia* (53a16); but a serious moral flaw would be precisely the wickedness that Aristotle has ruled out. To avoid this inconsistency some interpreters have concluded that *hamartia* has no moral content at all. On this view, Aristotle is referring exclusively to intellectual errors – to ignorance and mistakes of fact. This dovetails well with his account of reversal and recognition; both arise out of a misinterpretation of the circumstances in which a person is acting. So error in this sense is central to the complex plots which Aristotle favours.

But this interpretation of *hamartia* is too restricted. First, the assumption that moral and intellectual errors can be sharply distinguished is not correct. I might get an arithmetical calculation wrong because I am not paying attention; if I am an engineer designing a bridge, that negligence clearly has a moral as well as an intellectual dimension. If a bridge collapses with great loss of life because of an engineer's negligent calculation, the moral aspect of this error is serious; but this does not necessarily mean that the engineer is a wicked person. We can imagine circumstances under which the negligence, though blameworthy, is understandable. Suppose that he had just been told that he had terminal cancer: he *ought* to have taken more care, but we can understand his failure to do so. Secondly, it is possible to construct situations in which someone who knows what he or she is doing, and so is not subject to any intellectual error, does something they ought not to do, but understandably so. Perhaps they give way to intolerable pressure or provocation. The circumstances under which they act therefore mitigate the moral error in some way. The error may still be a serious one, in the sense that it has disastrous consequences; but the mitigating circumstances mean that it does not express a serious flaw in their moral character.

*Hamartia*, then, includes errors made in ignorance or through mis-judgement; but it will also include moral errors of a kind which do not imply wickedness. Aristotle's attempt to prescribe the best kind of tragic plot is therefore not as narrowly prescriptive as it may seem at first sight. His procedure is negative. He excludes various kinds of plot which he thinks demonstrably less than ideal; but that leaves considerable scope for diversity. The change to bad fortune must come about because of a *hamartia* (that is, not deservedly); but since *hamartia* can take a variety of forms, the best kind of tragic plot is not narrowly prescribed.

Aristotle's starting-point in chapter 14 is the relationship between characters. The tragic effect is enhanced when people inflict harm on those 'closely connected with them'. This rather clumsy expression (which we met also in chapter 11, in connection with recognition) is an attempt to render the Greek word *philos*, conventionally translated as 'friend' but in reality of much wider application. One's *philoi* include all those to whom one is bound by ties of mutual obligation – above all, the members of one's own family. The obligation to help friends and family, to protect them and to promote their interests, is one of the most fundamental principles of ancient Greek ethics; indeed, a common summary of virtue (that is, of the kind of behaviour most to be admired) was 'help your friends, harm your enemies'. Aristotle's point, then, is that a tragic plot is more likely to evoke fear and pity if a person inflicts harm on a *philos*, someone close to them. His next step is to correlate this point with two other variables: first, whether the agent actually goes through with the harmful act or not; secondly, whether the agent knew what he or she was doing or not.

The reappearance of the idea that acting in ignorance of the true situation may be the basis for tragedy gives chapter 14 something in common with chapter 11, where reversal and recognition both in-volved this kind of misapprehension, and with chapter 13, where action in ignorance is one possible form of error. Furthermore, Aristotle argues here that plots based on ignorance are superior to those in which harmful action is either planned or carried out with full knowledge of the circumstances. He uses the same word (*miaros*) here as he did in chapter 13 to describe the suffering of an outstandingly virtuous person. When someone knowingly plans or inflicts injury on one of the people with whom he or she is most closely connected we feel disgust, and our sense of revulsion interferes with the emotions of fear and pity. It is better, therefore, to have the character act in ignorance; there is then no sense of outrage to interfere with our sense of pity. Indeed, someone who unwittingly harms a person close to them is to be pitied; so in these situations we can pity the agent as well as the victim.

The next step in Aristotle's argument is something of a surprise. It is best of all, he says, if the injury is planned in ignorance but the plan is not carried out. That is, it is better if the identity of the intended victim is discovered before the injury is inflicted, so that disaster can be averted, rather than after the injury is inflicted, when the disaster can only be mourned. In chapter 13 the best plot is one in which a moderately virtuous person moved from good fortune to bad fortune. The second-best plot is the kind which has a double line of development, with the good characters ultimately enjoying good fortune, while the bad characters end up in misfortune. A play of this kind might dramatize a conflict between a good character and a bad character. For example, the good character may start off in bad fortune because he or she is oppressed by the bad character; this kind of play will evoke fear and pity because of the good character's initial misery. Or one could imagine plots in which fear and pity are evoked by the apparent imminence of a fall into misery, which is averted at the last moment. Plots like these will excite the tragic emotions in spite of their happy ending, since the characters we sympathize with pass through or anticipate misfortune; but they are not, according to the analysis in chapter 13, the best kind of tragic plot. In chapter 14, by contrast, the best kind is precisely one in which a change to bad fortune is imminent but does not occur.

Aristotle's two lines of argument therefore reach different, and apparently inconsistent, conclusions. Since there is an explicit cross-reference from chapter 14 (54a9) back to chapter 13 (53a18–22), there is little doubt that he meant the two chapters to stand together, despite the seeming inconsistency. This paradox has not been satisfactorily explained. If we insist that there is one kind of tragic plot that is best, then the two chapters are contradictory. But we have already seen that the concept of error in chapter 13 is designedly open-ended, and, on the assumption that there may be a variety of excellent tragic plots, the two chapters could be allowed to reach different conclusions without contradiction. It must be conceded, however, that Aristotle has not presented his arguments in this light.

## 8. *The pleasures of tragedy*

In the introduction to chapter 14 Aristotle says the tragic poet 'should not seek every pleasure from tragedy, but the one that is characteristic of it' (53b10f.); that is, he continues, 'the poet should produce the pleasure which comes from pity and fear, and should do so by means of imitation'. This stress on the characteristic pleasure (*oikeia hêdonê*) of tragedy has two functions. First, it serves to distinguish what is appropriate to tragedy from what is appropriate to other forms of poetry; thus the second-best kind of plot in chapter 13, with a happy ending for the good characters, gives a pleasure more akin to the characteristic pleasure of comedy (53a35f.). Secondly, it distinguishes the characteristically tragic pleasure from other pleasures which tragedy arouses, but which are not distinctive to it. We return here, therefore, to a point made earlier (§1): that Aristotle's analysis of what tragedy offers to its audiences is complex and multi-layered.

We start on relatively firm ground. In the definition of tragedy at the beginning of chapter 6 Aristotle says that tragedy is composed in 'language made pleasurable' (49b25), which is explained as speech with rhythm and (in some parts) melody. The fact that tragedy is written in verse, and that part of it is sung, gives us pleasure. This is consistent with the observation in chapter 4 that rhythm and melody are natural to human beings (48b20f.); for Aristotle 'natural' implies naturally pleasurable. Likewise, at the end of chapter 6 song is described as 'the most important of the sources of pleasure' (50b16); and the pleasure to be derived from music is identified in chapter 26 as one of the points in which tragedy is superior to epic (62a15–17). The same passage probably (it is not quite certain what Aristotle wrote) identifies spectacle as an additional source of pleasure. So there is pleasure to be got both from the verbal text of tragedy, and from its visual and aural realization – from what is seen on stage and heard when a play is performed. But these pleasures of the verbal text and performance are not distinctive to tragedy; they are present in comedy as well. And we have already seen that Aristotle rates lyric poetry and spectacle as the least important parts of tragedy.

Another pleasure is implied by the discussion of poetry as imitation at the beginning of chapter 4 (§2). Aristotle observes that imitation is naturally pleasurable to human beings, and explains this with reference to the process of recognition which it involves (48b12–17). When we look at a picture of Socrates we have to identify it as a picture of Socrates; this exercise of our capacity to learn and understand is (in Aristotle's view) pleasurable. If tragedy is an imitation, then in watching and responding to a tragedy we must engage in a similar process of recognition and understanding. In the light of Aristotle's analysis of plot we can see that the process involved in watching a tragedy is somewhat more complex than that involved in recognizing a picture as a picture of Socrates. When we watch a tragedy we have to follow the plot, which means recognizing that the events are a connected sequence, and recognizing that this sequence corresponds to some universal pattern (i.e. that the events are connected in accordance with necessity or probability). But this is not unduly demanding, and the process will still therefore be inherently pleasurable.[14] This cognitive pleasure is, however, not

distinctive to tragedy; the same process of recognition and understanding the plot as a connected sequence of events is involved in
watching comedy. Nor does the cognitive pleasure come from pity
and fear; if the cognitive pleasure can be derived from comedy just
as much as from tragedy, it must be neutral as to the emotions
which accompany it. The cognitive pleasure is therefore, like the
pleasures of text and performance, a pleasure derived from tragedy,
but not its distinctive and 'characteristic' pleasure.

The next step brings us to a much-discussed, and probably insol-
uble problem: *katharsis*. This concept appears just once and fleetingly
in the *Poetics*, at the end of the definition of tragedy in chapter 6:
'effecting through pity and fear the purification [*katharsis*] of such
emotions' (49b27f.). It reappears at somewhat greater length in the
last book of the *Politics*; but there Aristotle says that he need give
only a brief account, since he has discussed it in more detail in his
*Poetics* (1341b38–40). The text of the *Poetics* as we now have it is
probably incomplete; internal and external evidence suggests that
there was originally a second book, including (at least) the promised
discussion of comedy whose absence we have already noted (§3). A
fuller discussion of *katharsis* may originally have appeared in the
missing book. But that is of little comfort; we must do our best with
the little we have.

The context of Aristotle's reference to *katharsis* in the *Politics* is a
discussion of various uses of music. For children, music has an educa-
tive function; for adults it has a role in relaxation and leisure; but it
can also be used to bring about *katharsis*. Aristotle's example refers
to people prone to 'enthusiasm', by which he means hysterical or
ecstatic frenzy such as that associated with certain religious cults,
like the cult of Dionysus. Aristotle observes that music which
stimulates their frenzy can have a calming effect on such people
(1342a4–15):

The emotion which affects some minds violently exists in all, but in different degrees, e.g. pity and fear, and also enthusiasm; for some people are

prone to this disturbance, and we can observe the effect of sacred music on such people: whenever they make use of songs which arouse the mind to frenzy, they are calmed and attain as it were healing and *katharsis*. Necessarily, precisely the same effect applies to those prone to pity or fear or, in general, any other emotion, and to others to the extent that each is susceptible to such things: for all there occurs *katharsis* and pleasurable relief.

So the relief that *katharsis* brings is pleasurable. A pleasure that comes from the *katharsis* of pity and fear is, at any rate, not shared with comedy. So the question arises whether this kathartic pleasure is the characteristic pleasure of tragedy.

In trying to make sense of the notion of a *katharsis* of pity and fear, one thing must be stressed: Aristotle does not think that emotions are bad things in themselves. In this respect his outlook differs from that of Plato, whose critique of poetry in Book 10 of the *Republic* is based in part on a profound suspicion of the emotions. One of Plato's complaints is that poetry arouses emotion, and in so doing increases our tendency to be emotional; but in his view we should be bringing our emotions under control, not strengthening them in this way (*Republic*, 605e–6d). Aristotle has a more sophisticated and reasonable view of emotions. They are not irrational impulses. They are grounded in our understanding, since an emotional response to a situation presupposes an interpretation of it (as fear implies an assessment of the situation as one that threatens pain or injury); and since such responses can be more or less appropriate to the situation, they are open to ethical evaluation. So there is an intimate link between emotion and virtue (*Nicomachean Ethics*, 1106b18–23):

For example, fear, confidence, desire, anger, pity and in general pleasure and distress can be experienced in greater or lesser degree, and in both cases wrongly. To feel them at the right time, in response to the right things, with regard to the right people, for the right reason and in the right way – that is the mean and the optimum, which is the characteristic of virtue.

Deficiency as well as excess of emotion is a deviation from the ethical ideal. If I am paralysed with fear at the sight of a mouse, my fear is inappropriate and excessive; that is a sign of cowardice. But if I sit nonchalantly in the path of an oncoming steam-roller, then my lack of fear is equally inappropriate and excessive; that is a sign of recklessness. Courage, located somewhere between cowardice and recklessness, recognizes real dangers and responds appropriately to them. It is appropriate to feel fear in battle; if you did not, you would be prone to act rashly, endangering your own and your comrades' lives. But this fear should not be overwhelming; otherwise, you might desert your post. So for Aristotle the crucial point is not, as it is with Plato, to suppress your emotions; it is rather to feel the right degree of emotion in the right circumstances.

So the *katharsis* of fear and pity cannot be understood as getting rid of those feelings. Nevertheless, Aristotle does talk about *katharsis* in quasi-medical terms in the passage from the *Politics* quoted above. In those subject to enthusiasm kathartic music brings about 'as it were healing and *katharsis*'; and all those prone to pity, fear or any other emotion enjoy '*katharsis* and pleasurable relief'. References to 'healing' and 'relief' imply that *katharsis* does in some sense put right something that is wrong with us. What, then, might it be that is 'as it were heal[ed]' through the *katharsis* of pity and fear, if not the emotions themselves? The obvious answer is: an *excess* of those emotions. The *katharsis* of pity and fear would (if this is correct) work on people whose disordered emotional susceptibilities make them prone to feel these emotions at the wrong time, in response to the wrong things, with regard to the wrong people, for the wrong reason or in the wrong way. By stimulating the emotion to which they are excessively prone, tragedy discharges the tendency to excess; it thus relieves the pressure which their disordered emotional make-up exerts on them, so that in ordinary life they will not be so prone to indulge the emotion in question. On this interpretation, *katharsis* does not purge the emotion, in the sense of getting rid of it; it gets rid of an emotional excess and thus leaves the emotion in a

more balanced state, mitigating the tendency to feel it inappropri-
ately. Why should this be pleasurable? From an Aristotelian point
of view any process that restores one to a natural or healthy state
is pleasurable (*Nicomachean Ethics,* 1152b11–20, 1154b17–19). If
you are prone to feel some emotion to excess, then you are in
an unnatural state; the disorder of your emotional condition is
analogous to having a disorder in your physical condition. When
you are thirsty, satisfying your thirst is pleasurable; when someone
has trodden on your toe, it is nice to feel the throbbing die away;
something similar will apply to the restoration of your emotions to
a natural or healthy state.

If this approach to the problem of *katharsis* is even broadly correct,[15] certain consequences seem to follow. The kathartic effect applies to someone watching a tragedy only to the extent that his or
her emotional state is disordered; the more prone someone is to feel
excessive or inappropriate emotion, the more benefit he or she
stands to derive from *katharsis*, and (presumably) the more pleasure.
This is obvious: if a process is like healing, it applies in particular to
those who have most wrong with them. But Aristotle would certainly not have accepted that everyone's emotional dispositions are
seriously disordered; even the quotation from the *Politics* shows that
he saw various degrees of proneness to emotions, and only a minor-
ity are violently (that is, excessively) prone to them. Given the close
connection between emotion and virtue, to say that everyone's
emotions were seriously out of order would for Aristotle be to say
that there were no virtuous people, which is absurd. So *katharsis*
will not apply, or will not apply in the same degree, to all members
of the audience of a tragedy; the effect will be least on those whose
emotional dispositions are least disordered.

This in turn implies that the kathartic pleasure is not the characteristic pleasure of tragedy. Aristotle believes that the better members of the audience are more responsive to the best kind of tragedy;
note especially, at the end of chapter 13, that it is 'the weakness of
audiences' which leads tragedians to prefer the second-best kind of

tragic plot (53a33f.). In chapter 26, when he is arguing for the superiority of tragedy over epic, Aristotle has to counter the objections of those who think that tragedy appeals to vulgar and inferior audiences; but if the characteristic pleasure of tragedy was one that had most appeal to spectators whose emotions (and, therefore, moral character) were significantly disordered, Aristotle's high regard for tragedy would be hard to sustain. Aristotle seems therefore to be committed to the view that the characteristic pleasure of tragedy is one which will appeal at least as much to the better and more virtuous members of the audience; the pleasure of *katharsis* does not fit this description.

This conclusion runs counter to the widespread assumption that the reference to *katharsis* in the definition of tragedy in chapter 6 is meant to state the 'final cause' of tragedy – that is, the end or purpose for the sake of which tragedy exists. But there is no reason to expect an Aristotelian definition to state the final cause of a phenomenon (important though that may be in a complete analysis of it); a definition states what a thing is – its essence (49b23f.) or form.[16] Thus the definition of tragedy (49b24–8) tells us what tragedy is in general terms ('an imitation . . .'). It then uses the matrix constructed in chapters 1–3 to differentiate tragedy from other kinds of imitation in terms of its object ('. . . of an action that is admirable, complete and possesses magnitude . . .'), medium ('. . . in language made pleasurable, each of its species separated in different parts . . .') and mode ('. . . performed by actors, not through narration . . .'). It is fundamental to an understanding of tragedy that the action which it imitates is one evocative of fear and pity (52a1–3, 52b32); so this too is specified, but it is also (and crucially, in the light of the Platonic critique of tragic emotionalism) explained that the evocation of fear and pity is potentially kathartic. A play which was likely to encourage rather than assuage a tendency to emotional excess would not, in Aristotle's view, be a properly constructed tragedy. To say that tragedy should excite emotions in a way that does not do ethical harm to its audiences is to state something about the essence of tragedy, therefore, but it does not imply that the regulation of emotions is the function or purpose of tragedy.[17]

On the interpretation that I have outlined, then, *katharsis* is not the function of tragedy, but a beneficial effect which tragedy has on some members of the audience. Aristotle has constructed a multi-layered defence against Plato's critique of the appeal of tragedy to emotion. The first layer is provided by his more sophisticated ethical theory, in which emotions are recognized as in themselves good; the Platonic premise that emotions should be suppressed as far as possible is denied. The second layer is provided by the premise that the effect of tragedy and its characteristic pleasure is most available to the best members of the audience; if that is so, then it cannot be the case that tragedy merely panders to the distorted tastes of the vulgar and emotionally disordered. But the audience of a tragedy is likely nevertheless to include people who are vulgar and emotionally disordered, and a Platonist critic might claim that there is a danger that tragedy will have a bad effect on them; even if tragedy does not deliberately pander to their distorted tastes, it may still be true that stimulating their emotions will increase their tendency to feel those emotions to excess in ordinary life. The final layer of the defence, therefore, is the contention that, even for these people, the emotional stimulus provided by tragedy is beneficial, because it can relieve and reduce the pressure towards emotional excess by which they are afflicted.

The characteristic pleasure of tragedy is therefore not to be identified with the pleasures of text and performance, with the cognitive pleasure, or with the 'pleasurable relief' of *katharsis*. The natural inference is that the experience of tragic emotion is pleasurable in itself. This is a paradox, since pity and fear are forms of distress (*Rhetoric*, 1382a21, 1385b31). But the paradox is one with which the Greeks were familiar; the sophist Gorgias had described the effects of poetry as 'fearful shuddering, tearful pity and a yearning that is fond of grief' (fragment 11.9). Aristotle could well take the paradox as a given in this context, since its resolution is a question for psychology rather than poetics. We can only speculate on what resolution of the paradox he would have favoured had he addressed the problem explicitly. Since it continues to exercise modern philosophers, it would perhaps be surprising if Aristotle had found a compelling solution.

## 9. *The other parts of tragedy*

The analysis of plot is Aristotle's main concern in chapters 7 to 14; in chapter 15 he turns to the second most important of the six parts identified in chapter 6, character. This was defined in chapter 6 in terms of choice (*prohairesis*). Character is imitated when what is said or (presumably) done reveals the nature of the choice that is made, and hence the underlying moral disposition of the person who is speaking or acting. So when Aristotle talks about character he is not talking about the quirks and details of someone's individuality, but about the structure of their moral dispositions in so far as it becomes clear through what they say and do.

It is not surprising, therefore, that the first thing he specifies is that the characters should be morally good – or (a qualification added a few lines later) that they should not be morally bad *unnecessarily*. The example given is Menelaus in Euripides' *Orestes*. Menelaus squirms out of his obligation to offer protection and assistance to his nephew Orestes, a *philos* (see §7) towards whom his obligations are particularly strong. This is 'unnecessary' presumably in the sense that the plot would have got along perfectly well if Menelaus had not been such a despicable character. If Menelaus fails to support his nephew, this may be because he is a coward or because he is self-seeking; but there was no need to make him a self-seeking coward. So Aristotle is not saying that tragedy must be populated only by virtuous people, but that the characters should be as virtuous as is possible given the demands of the plot.

This requirement must be seen in relation to comments made

earlier in the *Poetics* on the nature of the people involved in the action of a tragedy. Two passages are particularly relevant: chapter 2 (on the objects of imitation), and chapter 13 (on the moral qualities of the person who undergoes a change of fortune). Chapter 2 contrasted 'admirable' people with 'inferior' people (48a2). 'Admirable' (*spoudaios*) reappears in the definition of tragedy in chapter 6: 'tragedy is an imitation of an action that is admirable' (49b24); *spoudaios* is often translated 'serious' here, but Aristotle means an action involving the admirable persons (persons 'better than we are') specified as the object of tragic imitation in chapter 2. Like many terms of commendation and disparagement in Greek, *spoudaios* and its opposite embrace social status as well as moral qualities. Thus in chapter 13 it is stated in passing that the person whose fortunes change should be 'one of those people who are held in great esteem and enjoy great good fortune' (53a10), and 'inferior' recurs in chapter 15 in a clearly status-oriented context: 'there is such a thing as a good woman and a good slave, even though one of these is perhaps deficient and the other generally speaking inferior' (54a20–22). One cannot expect aristocratic nobility of character from persons of low status, but they can still be morally good in terms of status-related norms of behaviour; a slave can be a good slave – loyal, hardworking and so on. In tragedy he should be; by contrast the slaves in comedy (whatever their virtues) are likely to be disobedient, lazy, dishonest and self-seeking. Conversely, high-status characters such as Menelaus can be morally bad. Tragedy, therefore, is essentially concerned with people who are of high status and of good moral character; there will be peripheral figures (slaves and so forth) of lower status, but they cannot be at the centre of tragedy's interest and should at least be good of their kind; high-status characters in tragedy can be morally bad, but not if they are meant to be a focus for our pity, and only if and to the extent that the plot requires this.

The second of Aristotle's four requirements for character, appropriateness, is very close to the idea of character being 'good of its kind' which Aristotle has just applied to persons of low status. A

woman in tragedy should be a good *woman*; she should have the virtues appropriate to a woman, and only those virtues. The fourth requirement, too, is straightforward: characters should be consistent. This obviously follows from the requirement of necessary or probable connection. If someone in a tragedy acts inconsistently and unpredictably, then one cannot say that what they do follows necessarily or probably on what has gone before. The one exception is where we have been led to expect someone to behave unpredictably (perhaps because they are mentally or emotionally unstable, or are facing an irresolvable dilemma); then, as Aristotle neatly puts it, they are *consistently* inconsistent.

The third requirement is more difficult. Literally, Aristotle says that the character should be 'like' (in Greek *homoios*): like what? Aristotle has used this word twice before in connection with character. In chapter 13 he says that fear is felt for someone 'like us' (53a5f.); and in chapter 2 he uses the phrase for people 'of the same sort' as ourselves, as distinct from those better or worse than we are (48a4–14). But this creates a problem: in chapter 2 Aristotle says that tragedy is concerned with people *better* than we are, while chapter 13 indicates that tragedy's distinctive emotional response is concerned with people *like* ourselves. A passage near the end of chapter 15 may point to a resolution of the apparent inconsistency. There Aristotle compares poets to portrait-painters. Portrait-painters, he says, 'paint people as they are, but make them better-looking' (54b10f.). There is therefore a combination of likeness and idealization in portraiture; a painter might keep Cromwell's warts, but make them seem less ugly than they really are. In the same way characters can be made better than we are while still retaining some imperfections of character; in this respect they will be like us, despite the element of idealization. This would agree with the requirement in chapter 13 that tragic characters should be virtuous, but not outstandingly so. They are like us, in that they fall short of the moral perfection whose downfall we would find outrageous; but they still tend to the better rather than the worse (cf. 53a16f.).

Aristotle's discussion of character is superficial by comparison with the analysis of plot. Even less attention is given to the third part of tragedy, reasoning, treated almost parenthetically in chapter 19. Here we find that the concept has undergone a degree of expansion. In chapter 6 reasoning and character were paired together as the two bases of action: if I am a coward and perceive the current situation as dangerous, then I am likely to run away. Both my moral disposition (my cowardice) and my understanding of the situation (my belief that I am in danger) enter into the motivation of action. More formally, reasoning was defined in chapter 6 in terms of demonstrating that something is or is not the case, or making a general statement (50a6f., b11f.). The agent's understanding of the current situation is revealed by what he or she says: an assertion or denial about the particular circumstances ('this situation is dangerous', or 'this situation is not safe'), or a generalization ('it is dangerous to sit in front of moving steam-rollers'). When Aristotle talks about reasoning in chapter 19, the elements of assertion, denial and generalization are still present, but others have been added. Reasoning here includes speech in which the characters arouse emotion, or make things look important or unimportant (55b37–56a2). In other words, it has extended to cover all the ways in which in a tragedy one person can use language to influence another. It includes now, not just the observation that it is dangerous to sit in front of a steam-roller, but also the persuasive devices which one character might use to frighten another with the prospect of sitting in front of a steam-roller or to convince them that it is not something to be entered into lightly. The techniques for this, as Aristotle observes, can be got out of the *Rhetoric*.[18]

From reasoning it is a short step to the language in which the reasoning is conveyed, and the next section (from the latter part of chapter 19 through to chapter 22) is concerned with diction. This may seem a generous allowance of space, in view of the comparatively low importance which Aristotle attaches to the poet's function as a maker of verses, as distinct from a maker of plots (51b27–9). On closer inspection, the material in these chapters does not seem so apposite. Chapter 20 is an essay on linguistic theory with no particular bearing on poetry. Chapter 21 is more directly relevant; it classifies various kinds of departure from standard discourse, and we learn in the next chapter that such departures from the linguistic norm are characteristic of poetic language. But even in chapter 22 it is striking that Aristotle is not concerned with the diction of tragedy in particular. It is tempting to infer that Aristotle, feeling that something had to be said about poetic diction, incorporated material which he had conveniently to hand even though it was not ideally adapted to its context.[19]

The section on poetic language concludes Aristotle's discussion of tragedy; in chapter 23 he turns his attention to epic. But there is clearly some unfinished business. Only four of the six parts identified in chapter 6 have been discussed; lyric poetry and spectacle have not received separate attention. Lyric poetry is a combination of words and melody. Its verbal dimension could conceivably be seen as treated implicitly in the chapters on poetic language, since their focus is not restricted to spoken dramatic verse; the musical dimension is perhaps passed over on the grounds that it is part of the realization of the tragic text in performance. A similar consideration applies to spectacle. As we have already seen (§4), Aristotle says at the end of chapter 6 that spectacle is not really integral to the poet's art; the tragic poet's job is to produce a text that can be performed, but the performance itself is a separate matter. Aristotle was certainly aware of the potency of performance; it is precisely that potency which tempts tragedians to rely on it to the neglect of plot, a tendency which Aristotle deplores in chapter 14 (53b7f.). That passage does not imply that the use of spectacle to complement and enhance the effect of a well-constructed plot is improper, and the comments at the beginning of chapter 17 on the need to visualize the action suggest that Aristotle recognized the importance of a poet's being aware of, and taking steps to enhance, the effect of his text in performance. One factor which may help to explain his reluctance to be more positive emerges from chapter 26, which shows that hostile

critics of tragedy saw performance as one of the objectionable
things about it; so Aristotle as a defender of tragedy had a reason not
to emphasize performance. In his reply to these critics he argues
that, since tragedy can have its effect without being performed, it is
not intrinsically more vulgar than epic; but he apparently goes on to
make the point that music and spectacle give pleasure (62a16f.).
Thus he concedes the objection to performance for the sake of
the argument, and shows that it does not entail the inferiority of
tragedy; but then he reverses the argument and claims that performance is a positive advantage. However, an oddity in the syntax
of the Greek at this point has led some editors to conclude that the
words 'and spectacle' have been inserted in error by a later copyist,
and that Aristotle mentioned only music; so we cannot in the end
be sure how positively Aristotle expresses himself about spectacle.

## 10. *Tragedy: miscellaneous aspects*

We have still not finished with tragedy. We jumped from character,
in chapter 15, to reasoning, in chapter 19; but there is a lot of material in between. This material is not bound to the framework of
the six constituent parts of tragedy established in chapter 6; its pre-
sentation is loosely ordered (at times, disorderly) and sometimes obscure to the point of unintelligibility. But it should not be neglected.
The material returns repeatedly to Aristotle's central preoccupation
with plot; but, by contrast with the broad issues of principle treated
in chapters 7–14, the emphasis in these later chapters tends to be
more practical. These chapters are, broadly speaking, concerned
with matters of technique, and so they sometimes look beyond the
design of the abstracted plot towards its concrete realization in a
play. Thus chapter 17 starts off from the perspective of a poet 'when
constructing plots and working them out complete with their linguistic expression' (55a22f.); chapter 18 includes comments on the
handling of the chorus (56a25–32).

It is no surprise that Aristotle's underlying concern with the connectedness of the events which make up a plot is repeatedly in evidence. For example, chapter 16 turns to recognition (defined in chapter 11) and classifies a variety of different techniques by which a recognition can be engineered. Since recognition is one component of the complex plot, which in Aristotle's view is more effective than the simple plot, this classification is not of purely abstract interest; the question of how best to handle one of the devices which do most to enhance tragic effect is an important and eminently practical one. Aristotle's classification works up from recognitions that are in essence accidental to those that are integral to the structure of the plot. Thus the least artistic kind of recognition is that prompted by a visible sign. Odysseus is recognized because he has a distinctive scar, but, as Aristotle implies in chapter 8 (51a25–8), his acquisition of the scar has no causal link with the plot of the *Odyssey*. By contrast, the best class arises by necessity or probability from the plot itself. In commending recognitions of this kind Aristotle picks up the idea stated at the end of chapter 9, that when something happens *both* unexpectedly *and* nevertheless as a necessary or probable consequence of what has gone before, this combination increases the audience's astonishment and thus enhances the emotional impact of events. This is important: Aristotle's preoccupation with necessary and probable connection is not the product of an abstract formalism; he believes that there is an intimate connection between the cohesion of the plot and the emotional impact at which tragedy aims.

The latter part of chapter 17 likewise explores some procedural implications of the theory of proper plot-structure set out in chapters 7–14. A tragedy aims to excite pity and fear, so a story is needed that will have a powerful emotional effect; we know from the discussions in chapters 13 and 14 which kind or kinds of story are most appropriate. Greek mythology is a rich repertoire of such stories, so it makes sense to turn there to find a suitable subject. We might look, for example, for a story involving acts of violence between close kin

(53b15–22). The most fundamental obligations of all are those of a child to its father and mother; so a man who kills his father or sleeps with his mother is doing two of the most terrible things imaginable. This would be the most potent material for tragedy one could hope to find. Oedipus, of course, did both of these things. So let us assume that we have chosen Oedipus as the subject of our tragedy.[20] Where do we go from there? What we do *not* do, according to Aristotle, is ask ourselves what was the first thing that happened to Oedipus, what happened next and so on. A historian might work like that; as we have seen (§5), historians in Aristotle's view are concerned with what happened, and so their narratives simply reproduce a given sequence of events. But Aristotle's poet is not concerned with what did happen, but with the kind of thing that would happen in accordance with necessity or probability (51a37f.). So we should not just take over a ready-made series of events as our plot. Having selected Oedipus as our subject, we ought (as it were) to forget about Oedipus and rethink the story in more abstract terms. Someone kills his father and sleeps with his mother; how can we represent this as something that would happen, necessarily or probably? In other words, how can we imagine this as part of a series of connected events? The poet is thus advised to work down from the most abstract possible formulation of the story of Oedipus through more and more concrete specifications of it until a final version is reached in which Oedipus' killing of his father and sleeping with his mother are embodied as a connected series of events.

How might we proceed? Since tragedy aims to evoke pity and fear we cannot have Oedipus do these things knowingly. Someone who knowingly killed his father and slept with his mother would be monstrously wicked; his actions would disgust us, and his downfall would evoke satisfaction rather than pity. So Oedipus must act in ignorance of the identity of his father and mother; recall here the significance of ignorance in chapter 14, and of error in chapter 13. Given Oedipus' lack of this knowledge, we can begin to see what is likely to be the climax of our plot: if Oedipus acts in ignorance, he must eventually find out what he has done, and the devastating impact of this discovery on him will be a perfect tragic climax; here the analyses of recognition in chapters 11 and 16 will be relevant. But the premise that Oedipus must be unaware of the identity of his father and mother also tells us something about how the early stages of the plot must be developed. His ignorance must surely imply that he was separated from his parents in infancy. Since the Greeks practised the exposure of unwanted infants, that is not a problem in principle; we just have to supply some motive for Oedipus' parents to expose him, and construct a mechanism to ensure that despite being exposed he survives to adulthood.

We have now embarked on the process which Aristotle describes as 'turn[ing] the story into episodes' (55b1f.). The abstract outline to which we have reduced the story needs to be converted into a series of concrete events, or episodes; and that series must be linked by necessary or probable connections if we are to satisfy Aristotle's requirements and avoid the defective plot-structure which he described earlier as 'episodic' – 'one in which the sequence of episodes is neither necessary nor probable' (51b34f.). Since the central events in our plot are to be Oedipus' killing of his father and sleeping with his mother, it would make sense to have those events drive the others. In both cases we can draw on supernatural assistance. If a baby is going to grow up to do such terrible things, a prophecy to that effect would provide the parents with a very strong motive indeed to dispose of their baby before he grows up; so we will postulate such a prophecy, and Oedipus will be exposed precisely because it is foretold that he will grow up to kill his father and sleep with his mother. But when he has done these things, he will be terribly polluted. In Greek religious thought, it was very dangerous for a city to harbour polluted persons; they could bring down disaster on the whole community. If this happened (if, let us say, a plague broke out) then the city would naturally try to identify the supposed source of the pollution in order to get rid of it; and this will give us a plausible mechanism for setting in train the enquiries which will lead to the discovery of the truth. Again, a prophecy can help us out here: the Thebans would naturally turn to an oracle for help in identifying the cause of their problem, and we can frame the response to point the enquiry in the right direction.[21]

Chapter 18 looks at the structure of a plot from another perspective. Complication and resolution (in Greek *desis* and *lusis*, literally 'tying' and 'untying') define the two stages of a plot hinging on the change of fortune which has been central to Aristotle's account of tragedy since chapter 7. The complication is everything up to the beginning of the change of fortune; the resolution everything from there on. So, for example, in Sophocles' *Oedipus* the change of fortune begins when news of the death of Oedipus' supposed father arrives and the truth about his real parentage begins to come to light; that point was already identified in chapter 11 as the play's reversal (52a24–6). Note that (to return to a distinction made in §5) complication and resolution are not parts of the play, but parts of the action which is embodied in the play's plot. The complication may include events which occur before the start of the play and which influence what happens in the play itself, but which are reported rather than enacted; in *Oedipus* everything involved in Oedipus' birth, exposure and survival, the circumstances under which he killed his father and married his mother, the onset of the plague, and the appeal to Delphi which that crisis prompts and which sets in train the enquiry that leads to the discovery of the truth – all this is crucial to the plot, but precedes the play's opening scene and is gradually disclosed to the audience as the play proceeds. One could, in principle, have a play which consisted solely of resolution; in such a play the change of fortune would already have begun, and the play would simply trace its completion and consequences (Aeschylus' *Persians* would perhaps be an example). The fact that Aristotle says that the complication includes what is outside the play and 'often' some of what is inside it confirms that he recognized the possibility of a play consisting solely of resolution.

If a plot consists of complication and resolution, then excellence in plot-construction (which, for Aristotle, is the key element of the poet's art) must embrace both parts. The comment, later in chapter 18, that 'many poets . . . handle the resolution badly' (56a9f.) harks back to a section in the middle of chapter 15, interrupting the discussion of character. According to the Greek text,[22] resolution should arise from the plot (54a37f.). That is, the poet should put together a sequence of events in which the change of fortune and its consequences are a necessary or probable consequence of everything that has gone before. It is an instance of the kind of unskilful resolution Aristotle mentions in chapter 18 when the poet has to resort to an arbitrary device to get the plot to work out the way he wants.

Aristotle's examples of arbitrary resolution in chapter 15 involve divine intervention. One is the end of Euripides' *Medea*. Aristotle feels that the playwright has created a situation in which Medea cannot be extricated from danger in any necessary or probable way; he has therefore resorted to the premise that the gods can do anything, solving the problem by the arbitrary introduction of a god-given flying chariot in which Medea can escape. Aristotle's rejection of this kind of device does not imply that divine involvement is inappropriate in general. One use of the gods which he explicitly approves is to convey information about those parts of the plot which fall outside the play. A god explaining the background to the play in a prologue, or a god appearing to foretell the future at the end of the play, would be typical examples. But there is of course much middle ground between the extremes of arbitrary intervention and the mere conveying of information. Aphrodite in Euripides' *Hippolytus* does not just appear in the prologue to convey information; it is her resentment which has set events in motion, and her intervention in human affairs is essential to the causal structure of the plot. There is no reason why Aristotle should object to this. Her intervention is well-motivated (she is angered by the way in which Hippolytus dishonours her), and its consequences follow by necessity or probability. To be sure, Aristotle did not believe in such deities;

but we know from chapter 25 (60b35–61a1) that the truth of the theological premises which poets use is not a matter of great concern to him. Hence he can accept unconcernedly the role which Poseidon plays in the plot of the *Odyssey* (55b18).

## 11. *Epic*

It should come as no surprise that Aristotle's first thought when he turns to epic in chapter 23 is about the structure of the plot. In epic, as in tragedy, the plot should be unified, with a beginning, middle and end suitably connected. The contrast between epic and historiography is familiar already from chapter 8 (where the contrast was with biography) and chapter 9; but a more complex set of contrasts is constructed here. The chapter begins by opposing unified poetic plots and defective plots with a quasi-historical structure. But it would be no great tribute to Homer to say that his plots are not defective; Homer is outstanding because he has handled plot-structure in the best possible way. To make the desired distinction between plots that are simply well-formed and Homer's unique brilliance in the handling of plot, Aristotle introduces a third element into the comparison. There are epics which have defective plots, constructed like works of history or biography about a single period of time or a single person irrespective of the causal connectedness of the events narrated; most epic poets write like this. Other epics have plots which are unified in Aristotle's sense, but which are very large indeed. An epic about the whole Trojan War would have been of that kind; it would have had a beginning and an end (59a31f.), and so been unified, but the vast mass of material in the middle would have made it hard to grasp the plot as a whole. In chapter 7 Aristotle stated that the upper limit on a plot is determined by what can be held in the memory; so this kind of plot, embodying a 'single action of many parts' (59b1), though in principle well-formed, would be pushing at the upper limit. By contrast, Homer selected a single self-contained part of the whole story of the Trojan war (the quarrel between Achilles and Agamemnon in the tenth year of the war). Although Aristotle does not make the point here, the same could be said of the *Odyssey*. A plot embracing everything that happened to Odysseus would not be unified (as we know from chapter 8). A plot embracing the whole story of his wanderings and home-coming would be unified; it would comprise 'a single action of many parts'. The plot of the actual *Odyssey* concentrates on the last stage of Odysseus' homecoming, skilfully using his earlier adventures in the way that Aristotle says the catalogue of ships is used in the *Iliad*, as 'episodes . . . to diversify his composition' (59a35–7).[23]

The beginning of chapter 24 proposes four overlapping types of epic plot. This classification is applied to the two Homeric epics: the *Iliad* is simple and based on suffering, the *Odyssey* is complex and based on character. The comment on the *Odyssey* is obvious enough: the poem is full of recognition-scenes, and the antithesis between good (Odysseus, his family and his loyal servants) and bad (the unruly suitors) makes character important. In chapter 13 the *Odyssey* was cited as an example of the 'double' plot which ends in good fortune for the good characters; so its happy ending contrasts with the suffering which pervades the plot of the *Iliad*, and which gives that poem its powerfully tragic character. On the other hand, Aristotle believes that complex plots are superior in principle to simple ones; so one implication of the attempt to classify the poems here must be that the *Odyssey* is, at least in this one respect, superior in its plot-structure to the *Iliad*, and by implication emotionally more powerful. Any reader who dissents from this conclusion should consider whether the fault lies in Aristotle's theory, or in his description of the poems. In the *Iliad* Achilles' actions lead, contrary to his expect-ation, to the very thing he least wanted – the death of his dearest comrade. There is thus a strong case that the *Iliad* exploits reversal, and that its plot is complex. Indeed, the centrality of this reversal to the poem's emotional impact could be seen as strongly supporting Aristotle's preference for complex plots.

The last part of chapter 24 returns to the theme of Homer's merits. Aristotle has already commented (in chapters 8 and 23) on Homer's skill in the handling of plot. Chapter 4 noted Homer's unique versatility (he alone worked on both sides of the bifurcation in poetry between imitations of admirable and inferior characters, composing both epic and narrative burlesque) and his adumbration of the dramatic mode: he lets the characters speak for themselves. The latter point rests on the high proportion of direct speech in his narratives, which Aristotle again singles out as an aspect of Homer's unique excellence (60a5–11). We may note here too that Aristotle is favourably impressed by Homer's powers of characterization: 'none of them are characterless: they have character.' Despite the priority which Aristotle gives to plot over character, he recognizes the contribution which character makes to the quality of a poem; and although the possibility of plot divorced from the imitation of character was recognized in chapter 6 (50a23–9), this statement about Homer confirms that Aristotle would not rate such a composition as highly as one with character.

There follows a section on astonishment and the irrational. Aristotle's theory of plot, with its strong emphasis on necessary and probable connection, tends to exclude irrationalities. If we apply Aristotle's criterion of good plot-structure strictly we will have to say that if all the events follow one another in accordance with necessity or probability, then the sequence of events is rational; if not, the plot is defective. Even Aristotle's approval of astonishment, as in complex plots with reversal, does not alter this; as he says at the end of chapter 9, the proper emotional effect depends on astonishment and connection together (51a1–6). But how strictly should Aristotle's criteria be applied in practice? One concession has already been made in chapter 15: there should not be any irrationality in the action, but if there is it should be outside the play (54b6f.). This implies that Aristotle would prefer a strict application of his criteria, but is able to tolerate a departure from them in certain circumstances. Chapter 24 notes that epic is more tolerant of irrationality because the action is narrated but not seen (we may recall here the comments at the beginning of chapter 17 on the poet's need to visualize the tragic action); since he goes on to say that irrationality generates astonishment, and astonishment gives pleasure, the implication is that it is legitimate for epic to exploit its greater tolerance of the irrational.

These two concessions have something in common. Irrationalities can be included in the parts of the action which lie outside a play, and in the action of an epic; in neither case will the irrationality be seen by the audience. Keeping an irrationality out of sight of the audience makes it less salient, and so helps keep intact the impression that everything is properly connected. The example of Mitys' murderer at the end of chapter 9 points in the same direction: an illusion of connectedness can have the same effect as connectedness itself (see §6). The next part of chapter 24, which says that Homer 'taught other poets the right way to tell falsehoods' (60a18f.), suggests a further way to smuggle an irrationality into a poem while giving the impression that everything makes sense. This is to exploit the human tendency to make fallacious inferences. (Aristotle's explanation suggests a fallacy of the kind: 'If Daisy is a cow, then Daisy has four legs; Daisy has four legs; so Daisy is a cow'.) If one is not alert and critical (the audience of a play or an epic recitation is likely to expect that events will be connected, and may not be in the frame of mind to focus on logical puzzles) then the fallacy may pass unnoticed; the poet will then have persuaded the audience by subterfuge that something is necessary or probable when it is not. Later in the chapter we read that one should prefer 'probable impossibilities to implausible possibilities' (60a26f.). Again, the emphasis is on maintaining the impression of connectedness: something that is (in reality) necessary or probable but which looks as if it is not damages that impression, and should be avoided; something which is not necessary or probable but which looks as if it is maintains the impression and is therefore technically superior. Here too a preference for having no irrationalities is combined with a willingness to tolerate them. Near the end of chapter 24 Aristotle seems to suggest yet another way to conceal irrationalities: you may distract attention from them by the brilliance of the writing, as Homer conceals the absurdity involved in the narrative of Odysseus' arrival in Ithaca 'with other good qualities' (60a34–b2).

Why, if Aristotle prefers the avoidance of irrationalities, is he willing to tolerate them? Chapter 25 suggests one answer: 'If impossibilities have been included in a poem, that is an error; but it is correct if it attains the end of the art itself . . . i.e. if it makes either this or some other part have greater impact' (60b22–6). Aristotle recognizes that an irrationality can enhance the effect of a poem, provided that it is concealed; in such a case he does not object. A poet designing a plot should aim (other things being equal) at consistency with what is necessary or probable; but where the poem's emotional impact can be increased by a departure from necessity or probability, that departure is legitimate. Necessary or probable connection is desirable in general not for any abstract *a priori* reason, but because in practice it generally serves to increase the impact of events (52a1–6). So one should always retain the impression of necessary or probable connection by distracting from or concealing (in one way or another) the irrationality; but sometimes a false impression will be more effective than the real thing.[24]

Chapter 25, from which this point has been taken, is concerned with the objections people raise to poems, and with the range of possible responses or solutions to those objections. The principles it enunciates can be applied to any poetic form (some examples from tragedy are mentioned in 60a30–32); the discussion is attached to the section on epic because the critique of implausible, inconsistent and immoral elements in poetry had been most comprehensively applied to Homer. Books 2 and 3 of Plato's *Republic* collect a certain amount of such material; the fourth-century sophist Zoilus earned the nickname 'Homer's Scourge' (*Homêromastix*) for his nine books devoted to identifying faults in Homer's poems. The six books of Aristotle's *Homeric Problems* collected discussions of such problem

passages; chapter 25 offers an extremely condensed synopsis of this material, and is correspondingly difficult to interpret. Rather than pursue all the details, it may be more helpful to look at the general principles which Aristotle states and consider how they fit in with the rest of the theory articulated in the *Poetics*.

Aristotle suggests three general principles. The first is based on the object of poetic imitation: poetry is not bound to imitate what is the case, but can imitate what ought to be the case or is said to be the case. This looks similar to what is said in chapter 9: the poet is not tied down to real events, but can use invented plots as well. But this later passage is more radical in its implications. Suppose a poet constructs a plot in which a god inflicts terrible punishment on a human being who has given offence; is that necessary or probable? In reality, no; philosophers will tell us that this is not a true conception of divinity. But in terms of traditional Greek religious beliefs – that is, what is generally said to be the case about the way gods behave – the god's action is certainly necessary or probable. So the plot of a poem does not have to conform to the underlying universal patterns to which events conform in the real world; it is enough if it conforms to the underlying universal patterns to which events conform in some imaginary or fictitious world, such as that of traditional religion. Aristotle's second general principle is based on the medium of poetic imitation, language. We know from the discussion of poetic style in chapters 21 and 22 that poetry is distinguished by departures from standard speech; such departures can be used to answer objections if it can be argued that the objector has misunderstood one of the non-standard usages characteristic of poetic diction. Thirdly, Aristotle insists on a distinction between the standards by which poetry and the products of any other *tekhnê* are to be judged. This principle, of course, applies to other arts as well. If I am illustrating a zoology textbook, I ought to get the details of an animal's anatomy right and resist the temptation to draw imaginary beasts; if I am painting pictures to hang in an art-gallery, I can legitimately sacrifice strict zoological accuracy in the interests of the painting's balance or composition, and dragons and unicorns may be more piquant than warthogs.

The last chapter of the *Poetics* (or of the part of it that has survived) raises the question of whether epic or tragedy is superior. The way this question is introduced suggests that Aristotle is taking up an existing discussion, rather than proposing the question himself; this is confirmed when he summarizes the position of those who criticize tragedy. But we know already that Aristotle does have a view on this question. The history of poetry in chapter 4 treats drama as the fulfilment of the development of poetry: it is something which the quasi-dramatic mode of Homer's epics adumbrated, and when drama proper appeared it supplanted epic because of its intrinsically superior qualities (49a2–6). Aristotle, then, will be firmly aligned with the supporters of tragedy.

We have mentioned some of the criticisms which Plato makes in the *Republic* of poetry in general, and of tragedy in particular. More immediately relevant here is the second book of the *Laws*, where Plato develops the idea that the quality of a poetic genre is correlated with the quality of the audience that appreciates it. Small children like puppet-shows; older children like comedy; respectable adults like tragedy; but older men, mature and experienced, prefer epic (*Laws*, 657c–9c). The critics of tragedy to whom Aristotle responds make a similar assumption (61b27–62a4): acting out a role is vulgar, as the vulgar performances of actors and such-like show; the only reason tragedy includes this vulgarity is to communicate effectively to the low-grade members of the audience, who could not follow what is happening or respond to it without this kind of exaggerated acting; hence tragedy is designed to appeal to the lowest grade of audience. Without them, it would be possible to eliminate the vulgarity of stage-performance; but then, of course, you would have a kind of epic.

The premise that the quality of a poetic genre can be judged from the quality of the audience that appreciates it is one which Aristotle would have accepted in principle; in chapter 13 he said that *weak*

audiences encourage the degenerate tendency of tragedy to turn away from the proper tragic pleasure to one more characteristic of comedy (53a33–5). But he rejects the critics' other premises (62a5–18). Vulgarity of performance is not limited to actors; epic recitations can also be exaggerated and vulgar.[25] Conversely, performance is not essential to tragedy, since a tragedy can have its effect when it is only read; so if the performance of a tragedy is vulgar, that is a fault in the performance but not a fault in the tragedy. Moreover, the potential for performance means that tragedy has the elements of spectacle and song, giving it a range of additional pleasures which epic lacks.

Not all of Aristotle's arguments in this chapter are equally compelling. He goes on to claim that tragedy is superior to epic because it is more concentrated; pleasure is better concentrated than spread out thinly (62b1–3). The flaw in this argument is evident from the example he gives: Sophocles' *Oedipus* would not be effective if expanded to the length of the *Iliad*. But that is scarcely to the point. No one would deny that the *Oedipus* at its present length is superior to the *Oedipus* expanded to the length of the *Iliad*; the real question is whether the *Oedipus* at its present length is superior to the *Iliad* at its present length. Expanding a play to the scale of an epic does not show that tragedy is better than epic; it shows only that tragedies should not be expanded to the scale of an epic – which we know already, since Aristotle explained in chapter 18 that tragedies contain less material (56a10–15). Furthermore, two passages elsewhere in the *Poetics* are difficult to reconcile with Aristotle's assumption here that greater concentration is superior. In chapter 7 he said that, within the upper limit of length imposed by memory, the larger the magnitude of the plot the better (51a10f.); in chapter 24 he said that the larger scale of epic gave positive advantages over tragedy in terms of its grandeur and variety: 'similarity quickly palls, and may cause tragedies to fail' (59b28–31). It is not clear, therefore, that Aristotle has managed to give convincing form to this argument, or to make it consistent with claims made elsewhere in the *Poetics*.

## 12. *Comedy*

The loss of the extended analysis of comedy which the original *Poetics* probably contained makes it difficult to be sure what Aristotle's views on comedy would have been.[26] The starting-point must be the brief account in chapter 5: 'Comedy is . . . an imitation of inferior people' (49a32f.). As we have seen (§9), 'inferior' has both moral and social implications. The central figures of comedy will include the lowly persons (such as peasants and slaves) who are only peripheral in tragedy; and comic characters, even those of high status, will tend to behave badly. In tragedy, moral badness is acceptable in characterization only to the extent that the structure of the plot demands it; but comedy deliberately incorporates moral badness in its characters, since comedy aims to evoke laughter and 'the laughable is a species of what is disgraceful' (49a33f.). The response at which comedy aims is antithetical to that of tragedy. Tragedy aims to evoke pity and fear, which Aristotle defines as reactions to painful and destructive harm (*Rhetoric*, 1382a21f., 1385b13f.). Hence tragedy involves suffering, which is 'an action that involves destruction or pain' (52b11f.); but comedy eschews it: 'the laughable is an error or disgrace that does not involve pain or destruction' (49a34f.). If the story of Orestes were burlesqued in a comedy, it would not end with Orestes killing Aegisthus but with their reconciliation (53a35–9); the abandonment of Orestes' obligation to avenge his father's murder would be a laughable disgrace.

One type of moral badness is a tendency to abuse others, and the characters of many extant Greek comedies indulge in liberal and often obscene abuse both of each other and of real contemporaries. Aristotle took it for granted that comic poets would use slanderous and indecent language (*Rhetoric*, 1384b9–11, *Politics*, 1346b13–23). In the *Nicomachean Ethics* (1128a22–5) he notes a transition from the open indecency of older comedy to innuendo in more recent comedy, and comments on the greater propriety of the latter. It is sometimes assumed that this expresses a preference for comedy in the more recent style; in fact it only implies that the more recent style of comedy is a better guide to the standards of behaviour to be observed in everyday life. We know from chapter 25 of the *Poetics* that 'correctness is not the same thing in ethics and poetry' (60b13f.) and that 'in evaluating any utterance or action, one must take into account not just the moral qualities of what is actually done or said, but also the identity of the agent or speaker' (61a4–7); greater propriety is not self-evidently an advantage in a poetic genre devoted to the imitation of inferior agents.[27] Of course, Aristotle would have disapproved of an excess of vituperation and obscenity in comic abuse; but we have no way of telling what he would have judged excessive in a comedy.

A point which needs to be treated with some care in this connection is the contrast which Aristotle makes between comedy with 'universalized stories and plots', introduced in Athens by Crates, and the older style of comedy in 'the form of a lampoon' (49b7–9). The contrast of comedy and lampoon reappears in chapter 9, where the concept of universality is explained more fully (51b11–15). It should not be read as a contrast between the abuse of named, real individuals and ludicrous stories about fictitious characters. As we have seen (§5), universality in Aristotle's sense depends entirely on the structure of the poetic plot. If events are connected with each other in accordance with necessity or probability, they constitute a universalized plot (51b4–9); and there is nothing to prevent real events, or the actions of real individuals, satisfying this criterion in comedy any more than in tragedy (cf. 51b29–32). By 'the form of a lampoon', therefore, Aristotle must mean a disjointed series of jokes or comic routines with no necessary or probable connection between them; comedy is better if it links its jokes and comic routines into a connected sequence.

The requirements concerning plot-structure must be applied to comedy with due regard to the pragmatism which we have already observed in Aristotle's treatment of tragedy and epic. Indeed, in comedy the scope for legitimate departure from strict connection in accordance with necessity and probability is greater, since discontinuities in the action may have a comic effect. To allow such discontinuities in comic plots does not negate the contrast between the connectedness characteristic of comedy with universalized plots and the disconnected lampoon-like comedy which it superseded. Where there is nothing but disjointed jokes or comic routines, discontinuity has no comic effect; it is only in the context of a generally sustained impression of continuity that a particular violation of necessary and probable sequence will seem incongruous and laughable. But, again, we have no way of telling what Aristotle would have regarded as an excessive violation of connectedness in a comedy.

## 13. *Further reading*

This introduction began by mentioning some of the problems which the *Poetics* poses to its interpreters; it scarcely needs to be said, therefore, that there are many and very diverse alternatives available to the account which I have sketched in the body of the introduction.

Among other translations which might be compared and contrasted with mine, I would recommend in particular those by Margaret Hubbard, in *Classical Literary Criticism*, ed. D. Russell and M. Winterbottom (Oxford, 1972); Richard Janko's *Aristotle: Poetics* (Hackett, 1987); and Stephen Halliwell's *The Poetics of Aristotle* (Duckworth, 1987). Janko's version, which 'attempts to follow the original Greek closely, with minimal alterations for the sake of natural English', is especially suitable for close study, and has extensive notes on points of detail.[28] Halliwell's translation is equipped with a more discursive commentary.

Halliwell has also published an English translation with facing Greek text in the Loeb Classical Library (1995). R. Dupont-Roc's

and J. Lallot's *Aristote: La Poétique* (Éditions du Seuil, 1980) contains an introduction, the Greek text with facing French translation, and a commentary. The edition I have worked from is R. Kassel's Oxford Classical Text (Oxford, 1965; reprinted with a commentary by D. W. Lucas, Oxford, 1968); but with such a difficult text there is often great uncertainty as to what Aristotle wrote, and I have freely departed from the readings printed by Kassel where this seemed appropriate.

Humphrey House in *Aristotle's Poetics* (Hart-Davis, 1956) gives a short and accessible, though now somewhat dated, overview. The only full-length systematic study in English is Stephen Halliwell's *Aristotle's Poetics* (Duckworth, 1986; this is not the same as his commentary, mentioned above); chapter 10 provides a good starting-point for exploration of the history of interpretations of the *Poetics* and of its influence. Halliwell's book has a very different vision of Aristotle's project from mine; but it tends (as one reviewer put it) to 'float at an Olympian distance from the text', and the style makes it harder than it should be to get to grips with his arguments. By contrast, Elizabeth Belfiore's *Tragic Pleasures: Aristotle on plot and emotion* (Princeton, 1992), a book full of fresh ideas to think about and argue with, is lucid and exceptionally stimulating. Anyone who has read this book and Leon Golden's *Aristotle on Tragic and Comic Mimesis* (Scholar Press, 1992) will appreciate how radically contemporary experts can disagree on the interpretation of even the most fundamental concepts of the *Poetics*. The excellent collection *Essays on Aristotle's Poetics*, edited by A. O. Rorty (Princeton, 1992), also illustrates the diversity of approaches to the text currently on offer.

For a short general introduction to Aristotle's philosophy see J. L. Ackrill, *Aristotle the Philosopher* (Oxford, 1981) or Jonathan Barnes, *Aristotle* (Oxford, 1982); at greater length, W. K. C. Guthrie, *Aristotle: an Encounter*, the sixth volume of Guthrie's *History of Greek Philosophy* (Cambridge, 1981). Jonathan Lear's *Aristotle: the desire to understand* (Cambridge, 1988) offers a philosophically challenging approach to Aristotle's thought; the introductory chapter, which explains the book's subtitle, is particularly relevant to this introduction's starting-point.

For a broader perspective on ancient literary criticism I would recommend D. A. Russell's *Criticism in Antiquity* (Duckworth, 1981) and *The Cambridge History of Literary Criticism. Volume I: Classical Criticism*, ed. George A. Kennedy (Cambridge, 1989).

## 14. *Reference conventions*

Like many translators of the *Poetics* I have divided the text into sections and sub-sections to help the reader follow the structure of Aristotle's exposition. These divisions, and the accompanying section-headings, are not part of the transmitted text and have no authoritative status. Nor do they correspond to any traditional or commonly accepted way of dividing the text, so they are of no use in giving references. For this purpose the reader should note the two series of numbers in the margin of this translation, relating to the two conventional ways of giving references in Aristotle.

One series (in roman type) runs from 1 to 26: these are the chapters. The chapter divisions do not go back to Aristotle and are not always very sensible, but they do provide one convenient and commonly accepted set of 'broad-brush' references.

The other series (in *italics*) runs from 47a to 62b: these refer to pages and columns in the nineteenth-century edition of Aristotle by Immanuel Bekker. Bekker's pages were wide enough to have two columns; so each page is divided into columns a and b. Strictly speaking, the Bekker pages for the *Poetics* run from 1447a to 1462b, but the abbreviated form is often used when it is clear from the context that the reference is to the *Poetics* rather than to one of Aristotle's other works. It is possible to give references with great precision by adding line-numbers to the Bekker pages and columns (for example, Aristophanes is named in chapter 3 at 48a27); for this reason modern editions conventionally give Bekker page and

column numbers in the margins. There are usually about 38 lines in a Bekker column, although the number does vary.

References to Aristotle's other works are likewise given either by book and chapter, or by page, column and line in Bekker.

# NOTES TO THE INTRODUCTION

**1.** In recent times what are probably additional fragments of *On Poets* have been discovered on papyrus.

**2.** Aristotle was born in 384 BC in Stagira in northern Greece; his father was doctor at the Macedonian court. He went to Athens to study in Plato's Academy at the age of seventeen, and subsequently taught there. He left Athens in 347, and in 343/2 was appointed tutor to Alexander (later 'the Great') of Macedon. He returned to Athens in 335 to establish his own philosophical school, the Lyceum. Anti-Macedonian feeling forced him to leave Athens again in 323; he died the following year. There is no consensus as to when in Aristotle's career the *Poetics* was written.

**3.** A brief explanation of the conventions for referring to Aristotle's works is given in §14.

**4.** This was already a key concept in the discussion of poetry for Plato; see especially Books 3 and 10 of the *Republic* (392d–8b, 595a–608b).

**5.** For example, epic narrative is counted as imitation and historiographical narrative is not (if it were, versified history would be poetry, contrary to what is said at 51b2–4); since Aristotle assumes the concept of imitation without explanation or analysis, it is unclear what criterion underpins this distinction and what the rationale of that criterion would be.

**6.** Hence the references to prose in 47a28–b13; for Aristotle, imitations in verse and prose have more in common at the most fundamental level than do imitative and non-imitative verse.

**7.** The antithesis is, in one sense, false: human beings are by nature social (or, as Aristotle's dictum is most often cited, 'political') animals (*Politics*, 1253a1–18).

**8.** A similar point arises in chapter 9. Poetry expresses the universal, as a consequence of its plot-structure (see §5); this does not mean that poetic forms lacking plot-structure (such as lampoon) cannot be poetry, but they fall short of the ideal to which poetry aspires.

**9.** That spoken language is rated more highly than song reflects the reduced importance of the chorus remarked in chapter 4 (49a16–18).

**10**. Chapter 12 interrupts the analysis of plot with a brief summary of the standard parts of the text of a tragedy. It is awkwardly expressed, awkwardly placed (the reference to 'what has just been said' at the beginning of chapter 13 ignores it) and not very illuminating; some scholars have suggested that Aristotle did not write it, but that is probably wishful thinking.

**11**. Note that unity of action in the sense defined here is the *only* unity Aristotle is concerned with in the *Poetics*; the so-called unities of time and place are later inventions.

**12**. Our instinct when confronted with such a report would perhaps be to try to establish an implicit connection between events in order to make a proper story out of it (was Ben perhaps Bill's bank-manager?). Aristotle's criteria for a well-formed plot correspond to our desire to find coherent, intelligible sequences in events; the effort that has been invested in blocking such inferences in some modern literature is evidence of the strength of that desire.

**13**. It would be wrong to infer that Aristotle had no regard for history and the recording of particular facts. A huge effort in collecting historical and empirical data informs his works on (for example) politics and natural history. The study of particulars is a necessary precursor to the philosopher's attempt to discern the universal patterns which lie behind them; but it is only a precursor, and the universalizing cast of mind characteristic of philosophy has more in common with the way a poet must think in constructing a well-made plot than with the procedures of a historian.

**14**. In *Rhetoric*, 1410b10f. Aristotle significantly qualifies the thesis that learning is naturally pleasant: 'learning *easily* is naturally pleasant to all'.

**15**. *Katharsis* is such a controversial concept that this cannot be taken for granted; experts on the *Poetics* continue to produce radically diverse interpretations (see, for example, the books by Belfiore and Golden cited in §13), and there is no consensus view.

**16**. The 'final' and 'formal' causes are two elements in Aristotle's doctrine of four causes (or, better, four kinds of explanation); see *Physics*, 2.3.

**17**. It might be felt that tragedy must have a role in its audience's moral development if it is to be taken with ultimate seriousness. But from an Aristotelian point of view the goal of human existence is not moral formation, but the exercise of formed moral character. To be ultimately serious, therefore, tragedy should have a place in the life of morally mature individuals over and above any contribution it may make to their moral development.

**18**. Even here, Aristotle's thoughts return to plot. The poet who is constructing a plot in order to excite certain emotions in the audience is doing something similar to what a speaker does to excite those emotions in his audience. Unlike the speaker, the poet does this without explicit statement; he places a series of events in front of us, and leaves us to register for ourselves the fact that it merits pity. But the kind of thing the poet puts before us is exactly the same as the kind of thing the speaker would put before us explicitly to excite pity; the same things are pitiful in each case. So even in constructing the plot, the poet can learn from rhetoric.

**19**. These chapters can usefully be read in conjunction with the discussion of style in Book 3 of the *Rhetoric* (chapters 1–12).

**20**. Aristotle's example in chapter 17 is in fact based on Euripides' *Iphigeneia in Tauris*, which he cites as often as Sophocles' *Oedipus*, although the two plays are very different. It is a fundamental mistake to suppose that Aristotle's theory of tragedy as a whole is modelled exclusively on the *Oedipus*, or applicable primarily to plays of that kind.

**21**. The completion of this plot is left as an exercise for the reader.

**22**. The Arabic translation of the *Poetics* (itself derived from a ninth-century translation into Syriac) says that resolution should arise from 'character'; but this is almost certainly not what Aristotle wrote.

**23**. 'Episode' is an elusive term, used in a variety of ways in the *Poetics*. The usage here, in which episodes may be derived from events outside the plot, seems to be different from the one noted in chapter 17, in which episodes are parts of the tragic plot in their most concrete realization (55b1f.; see §10).

**24**. This pragmatic accommodation of general principle to the needs of particular cases is consistent with Aristotle's understanding of the relation between *tekhnê* and practice (see *Metaphysics*, 981a12–24).

**25**. The intensely emotional atmosphere of an epic recitation can be gauged from Plato's *Ion* (535b–e).

**26**. Some have held that Aristotle's views on comedy can be recovered from the *Tractatus Coislinianus*, a much later text derived (it has been argued) from an abridged version of the second book of the *Poetics*. This view has been defended most forcefully in recent years by Richard Janko (see §13). But few scholars currently accept this view of the tractate's origins; fewer still believe that in its present, severely mangled form much reliance can be placed in it as a source for what Aristotle wrote.

**27**. The imitation of such agents and their behaviour does raise a concern about its ethical effect on impressionable young people. Aristotle's response can be seen in *Politics*, 1336b3–23, where he exempts comedy from a general prohibition on slander but recommends that the audience be restricted to adults, who will be immune to its potentially harmful moral effects; younger people, whose moral character is still in the process of formation, should be excluded.

**28**. Janko includes the fragments of *On Poets*, and a hypothetical reconstruction of the second book of the *Poetics*; the latter should be treated with caution (see n. 26).

# SYNOPSIS OF THE *POETICS*

Chapter 1  1. INTRODUCTION
           2. POETRY AS A SPECIES OF IMITATION
           2.1 *Medium*
Chapter 2  2.2 *Object*
Chapter 3  2.3 *Mode*
           3. THE ANTHROPOLOGY AND HISTORY
           OF POETRY
Chapter 4  3.1 *Origins*
           3.2 *Early history*
           3.3 *Tragedy*
Chapter 5  3.4 *Comedy*
           3.5 *Epic*
           4. TRAGEDY: DEFINITION AND ANALYSIS
Chapter 6  4.1 *Definition*
           4.2 *Component parts*
           4.3 *The primacy of plot*
           4.4 *The ranking completed*
           5. PLOT: BASIC CONCEPTS
Chapter 7  5.1 *Completeness*
           5.2 *Magnitude*
Chapter 8  5.3 *Unity*
           5.4 *Determinate structure*
Chapter 9  5.5 *Universality*
           5.6 *Defective plots*
           6. PLOT: SPECIES AND COMPONENTS
           6.1 *Astonishment*
Chapter 10 6.2 *Simple and complex plots*
Chapter 11 6.3 *Reversal*

6.4 *Recognition*

6.5 *Suffering*

Chapter 12   6.6 *Quantitative parts of tragedy*

7. THE BEST KINDS OF TRAGIC PLOT

Chapter 13   7.1 *First introduction*

7.2 *First deduction*

Chapter 14   7.3 *Second introduction*

7.4 *Second deduction*

8. OTHER ASPECTS OF TRAGEDY

Chapter 15   8.1 *Character*

Chapter 16   8.2 *Kinds of recognition*

Chapter 17   8.3 *Visualizing the action*

8.4 *Outlines and episodization*

Chapter 18   8.5 *Complication and resolution*

8.6 *Kinds of tragedy*

8.7 *Tragedy and epic*

8.8 *Astonishment*

8.9 *The chorus*

9. DICTION

Chapter 19   9.1 *Introduction*

Chapter 20   9.2 *Basic concepts*

Chapter 21   9.3 *Classification of nouns*

Chapter 22   9.4 *Qualities of poetic style*

10. EPIC

Chapter 23   10.1 *Plot*

Chapter 24   10.2 *Kinds and parts of epic*

10.3 *Differences between tragedy and epic*

10.4 *Quasi-dramatic epic*

10.5 *Astonishment and irrationalities*

10.6 *Diction*

11. PROBLEMS AND SOLUTIONS

Chapter 25   11.1. *Principles*

11.2 *Applications*

11.3 *Conclusion*

**12. COMPARATIVE EVALUATION OF EPIC
AND TRAGEDY**
Chapter 26  12.1 *The case against tragedy*
             12.2 *Reply*
             **13. CONCLUSION**

*Poetics*

# 1 . INTRODUCTION

Let us discuss the art of poetry in general and its species – the effect 1
which each species of poetry has and the correct way to construct 47a
plots if the composition is to be of high quality, as well as the
number and nature of its component parts, and any other questions
that arise within the same field of enquiry. We should begin, as is
natural, by taking first principles first.

# 2 . POETRY AS A SPECIES OF IMITATION

Epic poetry and the composition of tragedy, as well as comedy and
the arts of dithyrambic poetry and (for the most part) of music for
pipe or lyre, are all (taken together) *imitations*.[1] They can be differentiated from each other in three respects: in respect of their different
*media* of imitation, or different *objects*, or a different *mode* (i.e. a different manner).

## 2.1 *Medium*

Some people use the medium of colour and shape to produce imitations of various objects by making visual images (some through art,
some through practice); others do this by means of the voice.[2] Similarly in the case of the arts I have mentioned: in all of them the
medium of imitation is rhythm, language and melody, but these may

3

be employed either separately or in combination. For example, music for pipe or lyre (and any other arts which have a similar effect, e.g. music for pan-pipes) uses melody and rhythm only, while dance uses rhythm by itself and without melody (since dancers too imitate character, emotion and action by means of rhythm expressed in movement).

47b The art which uses language unaccompanied, either in prose or in verse (either combining verse-forms with each other or using a single kind of verse), remains without a name to the present day. We have no general term referring to the mimes of Sophron and Xenarchus and Socratic dialogues,[3] nor to any imitation that one might produce using iambic trimeters, elegiac couplets or any other such verse-form. Admittedly people attach 'poetry' to the name of the verse-form, and thus refer to 'elegiac poets' and 'hexameter poets'; i.e. they do not call people 'poets' because they produce imitations, but indiscriminately on the basis of their use of verse. In fact, even if someone publishes a medical or scientific text in verse, people are in the habit of applying the same term. But Homer and Empedocles have nothing in common except the form of verse they use; so it would be fair to call the former a poet, but the latter a natural scientist rather than a poet.[4] On the same principle, even if someone should produce an imitation by combining all the verse-forms (as Chaeremon composed his *Centaur*, which is a rhapsody combining all the verse-forms)[5] he should still be termed a poet. So this is the way distinctions are to be drawn in this area.

There are also some arts which use all the media mentioned above (i.e. rhythm, melody and verse), e.g. dithyrambic and nomic poetry,[6] tragedy and comedy; these differ in that the former use them all simultaneously, the latter in distinct parts.

These, then, are what I mean by differences between the arts in the medium of imitation.

## 2.2 *Object*

Those who imitate, imitate agents; and these must be either admir-  2
able or inferior. (Character almost always corresponds to just these  *48a*
two categories, since everyone is differentiated in character by
defect or excellence.) Alternatively they must be better people than
we are, or worse, or of the same sort (compare painters: Polygnotus
portrayed better people, Pauson worse people, Dionysius people
similar to us).[7] So it is clear that each of the kinds of imitation mentioned above will exhibit these differences, and will be distinguished
by the imitation of distinct objects in this way. These dissimilarities
are possible in dance and in music for pipe or lyre, and also in connection with language and unaccompanied verse (for example,
Homer imitates better people; Cleophon people similar to us; Hegemon of Thasos, who invented parodies, or Nicochares, the author
of the *Deiliad*, worse people);[8] similarly in connection with dithy-
rambs and nomes (one could imitate as Timotheus and Philoxenus
did the Cyclopes).[9] The very same difference distinguishes tragedy
and comedy from each other; the latter aims to imitate people worse
than our contemporaries, the former better.

## 2.3 *Mode*

A third difference between them is the mode in which one may imi-  3
tate each of these objects. It is possible to imitate the same objects in
the same medium sometimes by narrating (either using a different
*persona*, as in Homer's poetry,[10] or as the same person without variation), or else with all the imitators as agents and engaged in activity.

So imitation can be differentiated in these three respects, as we
said at the outset: medium, object and mode. So in one respect
Sophocles would be the same kind of imitator as Homer, since both
imitate admirable people, but in another the same as Aristophanes,

POETICS

since both imitate agents and people doing things.[11] This is the reason – some say – for the term 'drama': i.e. that the poets imitate people doing things. It is in consequence of this too that the Dorians lay claim to tragedy and comedy. The Megarians lay claim to comedy – both those on the mainland (who allege that it arose in the period of their democracy), and those in Sicily (that being the birthplace of the poet Epicharmus, who was much earlier than Chionides and Magnes); and some of the Peloponnesians lay claim to tragedy. They use the names as evidence. They say that they call outlying villages *kômai*, while Athenians call them *dêmoi*, the assumption being that comedians were so-called not from the revel or *kômos*, but because they toured the villages when expelled from the town in disgrace. And they say that they use the term *dran* for 'do', the Athenians *prattein*.

48b

So much, then, for the number of ways in which imitation is differentiated, and what they are.

## 3 . THE ANTHROPOLOGY AND HISTORY OF POETRY

### 3.1 *Origins*

4  In general, two causes seem likely to have given rise to the art of poetry, both of them natural.[12]

Imitation comes naturally to human beings from childhood (and in this they differ from other animals, i.e. in having a strong propensity to imitation and in learning their earliest lessons through imitation); so does the universal pleasure in imitations. What happens in practice is evidence of this: we take delight in viewing the most accurate possible images of objects which in themselves cause distress when we see them (e.g. the shapes of the lowest species of animal, and corpses). The reason for this is that understanding is extremely pleasant, not just for philosophers but for others too in the same way, despite their limited capacity for it. This is the reason why people take delight in seeing images; what happens is that as they view them they come to understand and work out what each thing is (e.g. 'This is so-and-so'). If one happens not to have seen the thing before, it will not give pleasure as an imitation, but because of its execution or colour, or for some other reason.

Given, then, that imitation is natural to us, and also melody and rhythm (it being obvious that verse-forms are segments of rhythm),[13] from the beginning those who had the strongest natural inclination towards these things generated poetry out of improvised activities by a process of gradual innovation.

## 3.2 Early history

Poetry bifurcated in accordance with the corresponding kinds of character: more serious-minded people imitated fine actions, i.e. those of fine persons; more trivial people imitated those of inferior persons (the latter at first composing invectives, while the others composed hymns and encomia). We are not in a position to identify a poem of the latter kind[14] by any of the poets who preceded Homer, although they are likely to have been numerous; but beginning with Homer we can do so (e.g. his *Margites* and similar poems). Because of its suitability, the iambic verse-form developed in these poems; indeed, the reason it is now called 'iambic' is that they wrote lampoons or *iamboi* against each other in that verse-form. And so some of the ancients became composers of heroic poetry, others of lampoons. But just as Homer was the outstanding poet of the serious kind, since he did not just compose well but also made his imitations dramatic,[15] so too he was the first to adumbrate the form of comedy; what he composed was not an invective, but a dramatization of the laughable. His *Margites* stands in the same relation to comedy as the

49a *Iliad* and *Odyssey* do to tragedy. When tragedy and comedy made their appearance those who inclined towards either kind of poetry became, in accordance with their nature, poets of comedy (instead of lampoons) or of tragedy (instead of epic), because these forms were greater and more highly esteemed than the others.

## 3.3 *Tragedy*

This is not the place for a detailed investigation of whether or not tragedy is now sufficiently developed with respect to its formal constituents (judged both in its own right and in relation to theatrical performances). But originally it developed from improvisations. (This is true of tragedy, and also of comedy: the former arose from the leaders of the dithyramb, the latter from the leaders of the phallic songs which are still customary even now in many cities.)[16] Then tragedy was gradually enhanced as people developed each new aspect of it that came to light. After undergoing many transformations tragedy came to rest, because it had attained its natural state.

The number of actors was increased from one to two by Aeschylus, who also reduced the choral parts and made the spoken word play the leading role; the third actor and scene-painting were introduced by Sophocles. In addition, the magnitude increased from short plots; and in place of comic diction, as a consequence of a change from the satyric style,[17] tragedy acquired dignity at a late stage, and the iambic verse-form was adopted instead of the trochaic tetrameter. (They used tetrameters at first because the composition was satyric in manner, and more akin to dance. But when speech was introduced nature itself found the appropriate form of verse, iambic being the verse-form closest to speech. There is evidence of this: we speak iambics in conversation with each other very often, but rarely dactylic hexameters – and only when we depart from the normal conversational tone.)[18] As for the number of episodes and other such features, the way each of them is said to have been elaborated may be taken as read; it would probably be a major undertaking to go through them all individually.

## 3.4 *Comedy*

Comedy is (as we have said) an imitation of inferior people – not, 5 however, with respect to every kind of defect: the laughable is a species of what is disgraceful. The laughable is an error or disgrace that does not involve pain or destruction; for example, a comic mask is ugly and distorted, but does not involve pain.[19]

The transformations which tragedy has undergone, and those responsible for them, have not been forgotten; but, because it was not taken seriously, little attention was paid to comedy at first. Indeed, it 49b was relatively late that the archon first granted a comic chorus;[20] before that the performers were volunteers. So comedy already had some of its features before there is any mention of those identified as comic poets, and it is not known who introduced masks, prologues, the number of actors and so forth. But plot-construction came originally from Sicily; among Athenian poets it was Crates who first abandoned the form of a lampoon and began to construct universalized stories and plots.[21]

## 3.5 *Epic*

Epic poetry corresponds to tragedy in so far as it is an imitation in verse of admirable people. But they differ in that epic uses one verse-form alone, and is narrative. They also differ in length, since tragedy tries so far as possible to keep within a single day, or not to exceed it by much, whereas epic is unrestricted in time, and differs in this respect. (At first, however, people used to make no distinction between tragedy and epic in this respect.)

Some of the component parts are common to both, others are

peculiar to tragedy. Consequently anyone who understands what is good and bad in tragedy also understands about epic, since anything that epic poetry has is also present in tragedy, but what is present in tragedy is not all in epic poetry.

# 4. TRAGEDY: DEFINITION AND ANALYSIS

## 4.1 *Definition*

6 We shall discuss the art of imitation in hexameter verse and comedy later;[22] as for tragedy, let us resume the discussion by stating the definition of its essence on the basis of what has already been said.

Tragedy is an imitation of an action that is admirable, complete and possesses magnitude; in language made pleasurable, each of its species separated in different parts; performed by actors, not through narration; effecting through pity and fear the purification[23] of such emotions.

(By 'language made pleasurable' I mean that which possesses rhythm and melody, i.e. song. By the separation of its species I mean that some parts are composed in verse alone; others by contrast make use of song.)

## 4.2 *Component parts*

Since the imitation is performed by actors, it follows first of all that the management of the *spectacle* must be a component part of tragedy. Then there is *lyric poetry* and *diction*, since these are the medium in which the actors perform the imitation. (By 'diction' I mean the actual composition of the verse; what is meant by 'lyric poetry' is self-evident.)

Now, tragedy is an imitation of an action, and the action is performed by certain agents. These must be people of a certain kind with respect to their character and reasoning. (It is on the basis of people's character and reasoning that we say that their actions are of a certain kind, and in respect of their actions that people enjoy success or failure.) So *plot* is the imitation of the action (by 'plot' here I mean the organization of events); *character* is that in respect of which we say that the agent is of a certain kind; and *reasoning* is the speech which the agents use to argue a case or put forward an opinion. 50a

So tragedy as a whole necessarily has six component parts, which determine the tragedy's quality: i.e. plot, character, diction, reasoning, spectacle and lyric poetry. The medium of imitation comprises two parts, the mode one, and the object three; and there is nothing apart from these.

## 4.3 *The primacy of plot*

Virtually all tragedians, one might say, use these formal elements; for in fact every drama alike has spectacle, character, plot, diction, song and reasoning.[24] But the most important of them is the structure of the events:

(i) Tragedy is not an imitation of persons, but of actions and of life. Well-being and ill-being reside in action, and the goal of life is an activity, not a quality; people possess certain qualities in accordance with their character, but they achieve well-being or its opposite on the basis of how they fare. So the imitation of character is not the purpose of what the agents do; character is included along with and on account of the actions. So the events, i.e. the plot, are what tragedy is there for, and that is the most important thing of all.

(ii) Furthermore, there could not be a tragedy without action, but there could be one without character. The tragedies of most modern poets lack character, and in general there are many such poets. Compare, among painters, the relation between Zeuxis and Polygnotus: the latter is good at depicting character, but Zeuxis' painting has no character.[25]

(iii) Also, if one were to compose a series of speeches expressive of character, however successful they are in terms of diction and reasoning, it will not achieve the stated function of tragedy; a tragedy which, though it uses these elements less adequately, has a plot and a structure of events will do so much more effectively.

(iv) Additionally, the most important devices by which tragedy sways emotion are parts of the plot, i.e. reversals and recognitions.[26]

(v) A further indication is that those who are trying to write poetry are capable of accuracy in diction and character before they can construct the events; compare too almost all the early poets.

## 4.4 *The ranking completed*

So the plot is the source and (as it were) the soul of tragedy; character is second. (It is much the same in the case of painting: if someone were to apply exquisitely beautiful colours at random he would give less pleasure than if he had outlined an image in black and white.) Tragedy is an imitation of an action, and on account above all of the action it is an imitation of agents.

Third is reasoning. This is the ability to say what is implicit in a situation and appropriate to it, which in prose is the function of the arts of statesmanship and of rhetoric. Older poets used to make people speak like statesmen; contemporary poets make them speak rhetorically.[27] Character is the kind of thing which discloses the nature of a choice; for this reason speeches in which there is nothing at all which the speaker chooses or avoids do not possess character. Reasoning refers to the means by which people argue that something is or is not the case, or put forward some universal proposition.

Fourth is diction. By 'diction' I mean, as was said before, verbal expression; this has the same effect both in verse and in prose speeches.

Of the remaining parts, song is the most important of the sources of pleasure. Spectacle is attractive, but is very inartistic and is least germane to the art of poetry. For the effect of tragedy is not dependent on performance and actors; also, the art of the property-manager has more relevance to the production of visual effects than does that of the poets.

# 5. PLOT: BASIC CONCEPTS

Given these definitions, let us discuss next what qualities the struc-  7
ture of the events should have, since this is the first and most important part of tragedy.

## 5.1 *Completeness*

We have laid down that tragedy is an imitation of a complete, i.e. whole, action, possessing a certain magnitude. (There is such a thing as a whole which possesses no magnitude.) A *whole* is that which has a beginning, a middle and an end. A *beginning* is that which itself does not follow necessarily from anything else, but some second thing naturally exists or occurs after it. Conversely, an *end* is that which does itself naturally follow from something else, either necessarily or in general, but there is nothing else after it. A *middle* is that which itself comes after something else, and some other thing comes after it. Well-constructed plots should therefore not begin or end at any arbitrary point, but should employ the stated forms.

## 5.2 *Magnitude*

Any beautiful object, whether a living organism or any other entity composed of parts, must not only possess those parts in proper order, but its *magnitude* also should not be arbitrary; beauty consists in magnitude as well as order. For this reason no organism could be beautiful if it is excessively small (since observation becomes confused as it comes close to having no perceptible duration in time) or excessively large (since the observation is then not simultaneous, and the observers find that the sense of unity and wholeness is lost from their observation, e.g. if there were an animal a thousand miles long). So just as in the case of physical objects and living organisms, they should possess a certain magnitude, and this should be such as can readily be taken in at one view, so in the case of plots: they should have a certain length, and this should be such as can readily be held in memory.

The definition of length which is determined by theatrical performances and perception is not relevant to the art of poetry; if it were necessary to perform a hundred tragedies they would time the performances by the clock, as they say used to be done on other occasions.[28] But the definition which agrees with the actual nature of the matter is that invariably the greater the plot is (up to the limits of simultaneous perspicuity) the more beautiful it is with respect to magnitude; or, to state a straightforward definition, 'the magnitude in which a series of events occurring sequentially in accordance with probability or necessity gives rise to a change from good fortune to bad fortune, or from bad fortune to good fortune', is an adequate definition of magnitude.

## 5.3 *Unity*

A plot is not (as some think) unified because it is concerned with a
single person. An indeterminately large number of things happen to
any one person, not all of which constitute a unity; likewise a single
individual performs many actions, and they do not make up a single
action. So it is clear that a mistake has been made by all those poets
who have composed a *Heracleid* or *Theseid*, or poems of that kind, on
the assumption that, just because Heracles was one person, the plot
too is bound to be unified. Just as Homer excels in other respects, he
seems to have seen this point clearly as well, whether through art or
instinct. When he composed the *Odyssey* he did not include everything which happened to Odysseus (e.g. the wounding on Parnassus
and the pretence of madness during the mobilization: the occurrence of either of these events did not make the occurrence of the
other necessary or probable);[29] instead, he constructed the *Odyssey*
about a single action of the kind we are discussing. The same is true
of the *Iliad*.

## 5.4 *Determinate structure*

Just as in other imitative arts the imitation is unified if it imitates a
single object, so too the plot, as the imitation of an action, should
imitate a single, unified action – and one that is also a whole. So the
structure of the various sections of the events must be such that the
transposition or removal of any one section dislocates and changes
the whole. If the presence or absence of something has no discern-
ible effect, it is not a part of the whole.

## 5.5 Universality

9 It is also clear from what has been said that the function of the poet is not to say what *has* happened, but to say the kind of thing that *would* happen, i.e. what is possible in accordance with probability or 51b necessity. The historian and the poet are not distinguished by their use of verse or prose; it would be possible to turn the works of Herodotus into verse, and it would be a history in verse just as much as in prose. The distinction is this: the one says what has happened, the other the kind of thing that would happen.[30]

For this reason poetry is more philosophical and more serious than history. Poetry tends to express universals, and history particulars. The *universal* is the kind of speech or action which is consonant with a person of a given kind in accordance with probability or necessity; this is what poetry aims at, even though it applies individual names. The particular is the actions or experiences of (e.g.) Alcibiades.

In the case of comedy this is in fact clear. The poets construct the plot on the basis of probabilities, and then supply names of their own choosing; they do not write about a particular individual, as the lampoonists do. In the case of tragedy they do keep to actual names. The reason for this is that what is possible is plausible; we are disinclined to believe that what has not happened is possible, but it is obvious that what has happened is possible – because it would not have happened if it were not. To be sure, even in tragedy in some cases only one or two of the names are familiar, while the rest are invented, and in some none at all, e.g. in Agathon's *Antheus*;[31] in this play both the events and the names are invented, but it gives no less pleasure. So one need not try at all costs to keep to the traditional stories which are the subjects of tragedy; in fact, it would be absurd to do so, since even what is familiar is familiar only to a few, and yet gives pleasure to everyone.

So it is clear from these points that the poet must be a maker[32] of plots rather than of verses, insofar as he is a poet with respect to imitation, and the object of his imitation is action. Even if in fact he writes about what has happened, he is none the less a poet; there is nothing to prevent some of the things which have happened from being the kind of thing which probably would happen, and it is in that respect that he is concerned with them as a poet.

## 5.6 *Defective plots*

Of simple plots[33] and actions, the episodic ones are the worst. By an *episodic* plot I mean one in which the sequence of episodes is neither necessary nor probable. Second-rate poets compose plots of this kind of their own accord; good poets do so on account of the actors – in writing pieces for competitive display[34] they draw out the plot beyond its potential, and are often forced to distort the sequence.     *52a*

# 6. PLOT: SPECIES AND COMPONENTS

## 6.1 *Astonishment*

The imitation is not just of a complete action, but also of events that evoke fear and pity. These effects occur above all when things come about contrary to expectation but because of one another. This will be more astonishing than if they come about spontaneously or by chance, since even chance events are found most astonishing when they appear to have happened as if for a purpose – as, for example, the statue of Mitys in Argos killed the man who was responsible for Mitys' death by falling on top of him as he was looking at it.[35] Things like that are not thought to occur at random. So inevitably plots of this kind will be better.

## 6.2 *Simple and complex plots*

10 Some plots are simple, others complex, since the actions of which the plots are imitations are themselves also of these two kinds. By a *simple* action I mean one which is, in the sense defined, continuous and unified, and in which the change of fortune comes about without reversal or recognition. By *complex*, I mean one in which the change of fortune involves reversal or recognition or both. These must arise from the actual structure of the plot, so that they come about as a result of what has happened before, out of necessity or in accordance with probability. There is an important difference between a set of events happening *because* of certain other events and *after* certain other events.

## 6.3 *Reversal*

11 A *reversal* is a change to the opposite in the actions being performed, as stated – and this, as we have been saying, in accordance with probability or necessity. For example, in the *Oedipus* someone came to give Oedipus good news and free him from his fear with regard to his mother, but by disclosing Oedipus' identity he brought about the opposite result;[36] and in the *Lynceus*, Lynceus himself was being led off to be killed, with Danaus following to kill him, but it came about as a consequence of preceding events that the latter was killed and Lynceus was saved.[37]

## 6.4 *Recognition*

*Recognition*, as in fact the term indicates, is a change from ignorance to knowledge, disclosing either a close relationship[38] or enmity, on the part of people marked out for good or bad fortune. Recognition is best when it occurs simultaneously with a reversal, like the one in the *Oedipus*.

There are indeed other kinds of recognition. Recognition can come about in the manner stated with respect to inanimate and chance objects; and it is also possible to recognize whether someone has or has not performed some action. But the one that has most to do with the plot and most to do with the action is the one I have mentioned. For a recognition and reversal of that kind will involve pity or fear, and it is a basic premise that tragedy is an imitation of ac- *52b* tions of this kind. Moreover, bad fortune or good fortune will be the outcome in such cases.

Since the recognition is a recognition of some person or persons, some involve the recognition of one person only on the part of the other, when it is clear who the other is; but sometimes there must be a recognition on both sides (e.g. Iphigeneia is recognized by Orestes from the sending of the letter, but the recognition of Orestes by Iphigeneia had to be different).[39]

## 6.5 *Suffering*

So there are these two parts of the plot – reversal and recognition; a third is suffering. Of these, reversal and recognition have already been discussed; *suffering* is an action that involves destruction or pain (e.g. deaths in full view, extreme agony, woundings and so on).

## 6.6 *Quantitative parts of tragedy*

We have already mentioned the component parts of tragedy which 12 should be regarded as its formal elements. In quantitative terms, the separate parts into which it is divided are as follows: prologue; episode; finale; choral parts, comprising entry-song and ode – these are common to all tragedies, while songs from the stage and dirges are found only in some.

The *prologue* is the whole part of a tragedy before the entry-song of the chorus; an *episode* is a whole part of a tragedy between whole choral songs; the *finale* is the whole part of a tragedy after which there is no choral song. Of the choral part, the *entry-song* is the first whole utterance of a chorus; an *ode* is a choral song without anapaests or trochaics; a *dirge* is a lament shared by the chorus and from the stage.

We have already mentioned the component parts of tragedy which should be regarded as its formal elements. In quantitative terms, the separate parts into which it is divided are these.[40]

# 7. THE BEST KINDS OF TRAGIC PLOT

## 7.1 *First introduction*

13  What, then, should one aim at and what should one avoid in constructing plots? What is the source of the effect at which tragedy aims? These are the topics which would naturally follow on from what has just been said.

## 7.2 *First deduction*

The construction of the best tragedy should be complex rather than simple; and it should also be an imitation of events that evoke fear and pity, since that is the distinctive feature of this kind of imitation. So it is clear first of all that decent men should not be seen undergoing a change from good fortune to bad fortune – this does not evoke fear or pity, but disgust. Nor should depraved people be seen undergoing a change from bad fortune to good fortune – this is the least tragic of all: it has none of the right effects, since it is neither agreeable, nor does it evoke pity or fear. Nor again should a very 53a wicked person fall from good fortune to bad fortune – that kind of structure would be agreeable, but would not excite pity or fear, since the one has to do with someone who is suffering undeservedly, the other with someone who is like ourselves (I mean, pity has to do with the undeserving sufferer, fear with the person like us); so what happens will evoke neither pity nor fear.

We are left, therefore, with the person intermediate between these. This is the sort of person who is not outstanding in moral excellence or justice; on the other hand, the change to bad fortune which he undergoes is not due to any moral defect or depravity, but to an error[41] of some kind. He is one of those people who are held in great esteem and enjoy great good fortune, like Oedipus, Thyestes, and distinguished men from that kind of family.

It follows that a well-formed plot will be simple[42] rather than (as some people say) double, and that it must involve a change not *to* good fortune *from* bad fortune, but (on the contrary) *from* good fortune *to* bad fortune – and this must be due not to depravity but to a serious error on the part of someone of the kind specified (or better than that, rather than worse). There is evidence of this in practice. At first poets used to pick out stories at random; but nowadays the best tragedies are constructed around a few households, e.g. about Alcmeon, Oedipus, Orestes, Meleager, Thyestes, Telephus and any others whose lot it has been to experience something terrible – or to perform some terrible action.[43]

So the best tragedy, in artistic terms, is based on this structure. This is why those who criticize Euripides for doing this in his tragedies, most of which end in bad fortune, are making the same mistake;[44] for this is, as has been stated, correct. There is very powerful evidence for this. On stage and in performance people recognize that plays of this kind (provided that they are successfully executed) are the most tragic, and Euripides, even if his technique is faulty in other respects, is regarded as the most tragic of poets.

Second-best is the structure which some say comes first – that which has a double structure like the *Odyssey*, and which ends with the opposite outcome for better and worse people.[45] It is thought to come first because of the weakness of audiences; the poets follow the audiences' lead and compose whatever is to their taste. But this is not the pleasure which comes from tragedy; it is more characteristic of comedy. In comedy even people who are the bitterest enemies in the story, like Orestes and Aegisthus, go off reconciled in the end, and no one gets killed by anybody.[46]

## 7.3 *Second introduction*

14    It is possible for the evocation of fear and pity to result from the
53b  spectacle, and also from the structure of the events itself. The latter is preferable and is the mark of a better poet. The plot should be constructed in such a way that, even without seeing it, anyone who hears the events which occur shudders and feels pity at what happens; this is how someone would react on hearing the plot of the *Oedipus*. Producing this effect through spectacle is less artistic, and is dependent on the production. Those who use spectacle to produce an effect which is not evocative of fear, but simply monstrous, have nothing to do with tragedy; one should not seek every pleasure from tragedy, but the one that is characteristic of it. And since the poet should produce the pleasure which comes from pity and fear, and should do so by means of imitation, clearly this must be brought about in the events.

## 7.4 *Second deduction*

Let us therefore take up the question of what classes of events appear terrible or pitiable.

Necessarily, we are concerned with interactions between people who are closely connected[47] with each other, or between enemies, or between neutrals. If enemy acts on enemy, there is nothing pitiable either in the action itself or in its imminence, except in respect of the actual suffering in itself. Likewise with neutrals. What one should look for are situations in which sufferings arise within close relationships, e.g. brother kills brother, son father, mother son, or son mother – or is on the verge of killing them, or does something else of the same kind.

Now, one cannot undo traditional stories (I mean, for example, Clytaemnestra's death at Orestes' hands, or Eriphyle's at Alcmeon's);[48] but one has to discover for oneself how to use even the traditional stories well. Let us state more clearly what this involves. It is possible for the action to come about in the way that the old poets used to do it, with people acting in full knowledge and awareness; this is in fact how Euripides portrayed Medea killing her children.[49] It is also possible for the action to be performed, but for the agents to do the terrible deed in ignorance and only then to recognize the close connection, as in Sophocles' *Oedipus*. (This is outside the play: examples in the tragedy itself are Astydamas' *Alcmeon* or Telegonus in the *Odysseus Wounded*.)[50] A third possibility besides these is for someone to be on the verge of performing some irreparable deed through ignorance, and for the recognition to pre-empt the act. Besides these there is no other possibility: necessarily the agents must either act or not act, either knowingly or in ignorance.[51]

Of these, being on the verge of acting wittingly and not doing so is worst; this is disgusting, and is not tragic since there is no suffering. So no one composes in this way, or only rarely (e.g. Haemon and *54a* Creon in the *Antigone*).[52] Performing the action is second; but it is better if the action is performed in ignorance and followed by a recognition – there is nothing disgusting in this, and the recognition has great emotional impact. But the last case is best; I mean, for example, in the *Cresphontes* Merope is on the verge of killing her son but does not do it, but instead recognizes him;[53] the same happens with sister and brother in the *Iphigeneia*;[54] and in the *Helle* the son recognizes his mother when on the verge of handing her over.[55]

For this reason, as I said some time ago,[56] tragedies are concerned with a limited number of families. Although their search was guided by chance rather than art, poets discovered how to produce this kind of effect in plots; so they are forced to turn to just those households in which this kind of suffering has come about.

# 8. OTHER ASPECTS OF TRAGEDY

## 8.1 *Character*

Enough has been said about the structure of events and what plots 15 should be like; as for character, there are four things to aim at:

(i) First and foremost, *goodness*. As was said earlier, speech or action will possess character if it discloses the nature of a deliberate choice; the character is good if the choice is good. This is possible in each class of person: there is such a thing as a good woman and a good slave, even though one of these is perhaps deficient and the other generally speaking inferior.[57]

(ii) Secondly, *appropriateness*: it is possible for the character to be courageous, but for this to be an inappropriate way for a woman to display courage or cleverness.[58]

(iii) Thirdly, *likeness*: this is not the same as making character good and appropriate, as has already been stated.[59]

(iv) Fourthly, *consistency*: even if the subject of the imitation is inconsistent, and that is the kind of character that is presupposed, it should nevertheless be consistently inconsistent.

An example of unnecessary badness of character is Menelaus in the *Orestes*;[60] of impropriety and inappropriateness, Odysseus' lament in the *Scylla*[61] and Melanippe's speech.[62] An example of in-consistency is the *Iphigeneia in Aulis*:[63] when she pleads for her life to be spared she is not at all like her later self – but in characterization, just as much as in the structure of events, one ought always to look for what is necessary or probable: it should be necessary or probable that this kind of person says or does this kind of thing, and it should be necessary or probable that this happens after that.

(Clearly, therefore, the resolutions of plots should also come about from the plot itself, and not by means of a theatrical device, as *54b* in the *Medea*, or the events concerned with the launching of the ships in the *Iliad*.[64] A theatrical device may be used for things outside the play – whether prior events which are beyond human know-ledge, or subsequent events which need prediction and narration – since we grant that the gods can see everything. But there should be nothing irrational in the events themselves; or, failing that, it should be outside the play, as for example in Sophocles' *Oedipus*.)[65]

Since tragedy is an imitation of people better than we are, one should imitate good portrait-painters. In rendering the individual form, they paint people as they are, but make them better-looking. In the same way the poet who is imitating people who are irascible or lazy or who have other traits of character of that sort should por-tray them as having these characteristics, but also as decent people. For example, Homer portrayed Achilles as both a good man and a paradigm of obstinacy.[66]

One should observe these points closely, and in addition those corresponding to the perceptions that are necessary concomitants of the art of poetry. It is possible to make many mistakes with respect to these. But they have been discussed in sufficient detail in my published works.[67]

## 8.2 *Kinds of recognition*

16  We have already said what recognition is. Its kinds are:

(i) First of all, the least artistic kind (and the one which people use
most, because of their lack of ingenuity) is that by means of
tokens. Some of these are congenital (e.g. 'the spear the earth-
born bear',[68] or stars such as Carcinus used in his *Thyestes*),[69] and
some are acquired; of the latter, some are physical characteristics
(e.g. scars), others are external (e.g. necklaces, or the use of the
boat in the *Tyro*).[70] It is possible to make better or worse use of
these. For example, Odysseus is recognized by means of the scar
both by the nurse and by the swineherds, but in different ways.
Recognitions that are used only for confirmation are less artistic
(so too all recognitions of that kind); recognitions which arise out
of a reversal, as in the bath-scene, are better.[71]

(ii) Second are those which are contrived by the poet; for that reason
they are inartistic. For example, Orestes in the *Iphigeneia* revealed
his own identity; Iphigeneia's identity is revealed by the letter, but
Orestes declares in person what the poet (instead of the plot) requires. This brings it close to the error mentioned above: it would
have been possible actually to bring tokens with him.[72] There is
also the 'voice of the shuttle' in Sophocles' *Tereus*.[73]

(iii) The third is by means of memory, when someone grasps the sig-
55a    nificance of something that he sees. This is how it is in Dicaeogenes' *Cyprians*, where he sees the painting and bursts into tears,
and in the tale told to Alcinous, where Odysseus listens to the
lyre-player, is reminded of his past and weeps; recognition results
in both cases.[74]

(iv) Fourth is that which arises from inference. For example, in the
*Choephori*: 'someone similar has come; no one is similar except
Orestes; so he has come'.[75] There is also the recognition which
Polyidus the sophist suggested for Iphigeneia; he said that it was

probable for Orestes to infer that his sister had been sacrificed, and so it was now his turn to be sacrificed. Also in Theodectes' *Tydeus*, that he came to find a son, but is perishing himself. And the recognition in the *Sons of Phineus*; when the women saw the place they inferred that it was their fate to die there, since that was where they had been exposed.[76]

(v) There is also a composite kind arising from a false inference on the part of the audience. For example, in *Odysseus the False Messenger*,[77] the fact that he can bend the bow and nobody else is contrived by the poet as a premise, as is his claim that he will recognize the bow which he has not seen; and although he is going to make himself known by means of the former, he actually does so by means of the latter, which involves a false inference.

(vi) The best recognition of all is that which arises out of the actual course of events, where the emotional impact is achieved through events that are probable, as in Sophocles' *Oedipus* and the *Iphigeneia* (her wish to send a letter is probable). Only this kind does without contrived tokens and necklaces. Second-best are those which arise from inference.

## 8.3 *Visualizing the action*

When constructing plots and working them out complete with their linguistic expression, one should so far as possible visualize what is happening. By envisaging things very vividly in this way, as if one were actually present at the events themselves, one can find out what is appropriate, and inconsistencies are least likely to be overlooked. The criticism made of Carcinus provides evidence of this: Amphiaraus was coming back from the temple; this would have escaped the notice of anyone who did not see it, but it failed in performance because the audience was dissatisfied with it.[78]

One should also, as far as possible, work plots out using gestures. Given the same natural talent, those who are actually experiencing the emotions are the most convincing; someone who is distressed or angry acts out distress and irritation most authentically. (This is why the art of poetry belongs to people who are naturally gifted or mad; of these, the former are adaptable, and the latter are not in their right mind.)[79]

## 8.4 *Outlines and episodization*

Stories, even ones which have been the subject of a previous poem, should first be set out in universal terms when one is making use of them oneself; on that basis, one should then turn the story into episodes and elaborate it.

55b

As an example of what I mean by considering the universal, take the *Iphigeneia*: 'A girl has been sacrificed and has disappeared without those who performed the sacrifice being aware of it. Set down in another country, where it was the custom to sacrifice foreigners to the goddess, she becomes the priestess of this rite. It subsequently happens that the priestess's brother arrives (the fact that the god ordered him to go there is outside the universal; so too the reason);[80] on his arrival he is captured, but when he is on the verge of being sacrificed he discloses his identity (either as Euripides did it, or as in Polyidus,[81] by saying – as was quite probable – that it was his lot, as well as his sister's, to be sacrificed). Escape ensues.' After that, one should supply the names and turn the story into episodes. The episodes must be appropriate – for example, in the case of Orestes the fit of madness which resulted in his capture, and the escape by means of the purification.

In plays the episodes are concise, but in epic poetry they are used to increase the length. The story of the *Odyssey* is not very long: 'A man has been away from home for many years; he is kept under close observation by Poseidon, and is alone; at home affairs are in such a state that his property is being squandered by the suitors, and plots are being laid against his son. Despite being shipwrecked he reaches home, reveals his identity to a number of people and attacks. He survives and destroys his enemies.' That much is integral; the rest is episodes.

## 8.5 *Complication and resolution*

Every tragedy consists of a complication and a resolution. What is    18 outside the play, and often some of what is inside, comprises the complication; the resolution is the rest. By *complication* I mean everything from the beginning up to and including the section which immediately precedes the change to good fortune or bad fortune; by *resolution* I mean everything from the beginning of the change of fortune to the end. Thus in Theodectes' *Lynceus* the complication consists of events before the play, the seizure of the child and the disclosure of the parents; the resolution is everything from the capital charge to the end.[82]

## 8.6 *Kinds of tragedy*

There are four kinds of tragedy (since that was also the number of component parts mentioned):[83] complex tragedy, depending entirely on reversal and recognition; tragedy of suffering (e.g. plays about Ajax or Ixion); tragedy of character (e.g. *Women of Phthia*    56a and *Peleus*); and, fourth, simple tragedy (e.g. *Daughters of Phorcys*, *Prometheus* and plays set in the underworld).

By preference one should try to include all the component parts, or failing that most of them and the most important, especially given the captious criticisms which people make of poets nowadays. Because there have been poets good at each part, people expect individual poets to surpass the particular excellence of every one.[84]

The proper basis for contrasting and comparing tragedies is principally in virtue of the plot, i.e. whether the complication and resolution are the same. Many poets are good at complication but handle the resolution badly;[85] but both should be treated with equal care.

## 8.7 *Tragedy and epic*

Bearing in mind what I have already said several times, one should not compose a tragedy out of a body of material which would serve for an epic – by which I mean one that contains a multiplicity of stories (for example, if one were to use the whole plot of the *Iliad*). In epic, because of its length, every part is given the appropriate magnitude; but in plays the result is quite contrary to one's expectation. There is evidence of this in the fact that everyone who has composed a *Sack of Troy* as a whole, and not piecemeal like Euripides, or a *Niobe* and not like Aeschylus, has either failed or done badly in the competition; even Agathon failed in this one respect.[86]

## 8.8 *Astonishment*

In reversals and in simple actions poets use astonishment to achieve their chosen aims;[87] this is tragic and agreeable. This happens when someone who is clever but bad (like Sisyphus) is deceived, or someone who is courageous but unjust is defeated. There is no violation of probability in this; as Agathon said, it is probable for many improbable things to happen.[88]

## 8.9 *The chorus*

One should handle the chorus as one of the actors; it should be part of the whole and should contribute to the performance – not as in Euripides, but as in Sophocles. In the other poets the songs have no more to do with the plot than they do with any other play; this is the reason why they sing interludes. This is a practice which Agathon was the first to start;[89] but what is the difference between singing interludes and transferring a speech or a whole episode from one play into another?

# 9. DICTION

## 9.1 *Introduction*

The other formal elements have been discussed; it remains to discuss diction and reasoning. The discussion of reasoning can be reserved for my *Rhetoric*, since it has more to do with that field of enquiry. Under reasoning fall those effects which must be produced by language; these include proof and refutation, the production of emotions (e.g. pity, fear, anger, etc.), and also establishing importance or unimportance.

(It is clear that in the events too one should apply the same principles when it is necessary to make something seem pitiable or terrible, important or probable. The only difference is that the one set of effects should be apparent without explicit statement, while the others must be produced in speech by the speaker, and must come about through the spoken word. What would the speaker's function be if the necessary effect were evident without the use of language?)

As for diction, one kind of enquiry is into the forms of utterance; knowledge of these belongs to the art of performance and to the person who has that kind of expert knowledge – e.g. what is a command, prayer, narrative, threat, question, answer, and anything else of that kind. Knowledge or ignorance of these matters does not give rise to any criticism relevant to the art of poetry that is actually worth taking seriously; no one could suppose that there is an error

19

56b

31

in the point Protagoras criticized (i.e. that Homer thinks he is utter-
ing a prayer but is in fact giving an order when he says 'Goddess,
sing the wrath':[90] Protagoras' point is that telling someone to do
something or not is an order). So let us set that aside as an investigation belonging to an art other than that of poetry.

## 9.2 *Basic concepts*

20 Diction as a whole has the following elements: phoneme, syllable,
connective, noun, verb, conjunction, inflection, utterance.

(i) A *phoneme* is an indivisible vocalization – not any kind, however,
but one which can be part of a composite vocalization; some animal noises are indivisible, but these are not what I mean by phonemes.[91] Phonemes are classified as vowels, continuants and mutes:
  (a) a *vowel* does not involve contact between the organs of speech,
  and has audible sound;
  (b) a *continuant* does involve contact between the organs of speech,
  and has audible sound: e.g. *s, r*;
  (c) a *mute* does involve contact between the organs of speech, but
  does not have sound in itself; it becomes audible when combined with a phoneme which has audible sound: e.g. *g, d*.
Phonemes differ in the shape of the mouth, in the point of contact, in the presence or absence of aspiration, in length or brevity,
and in acute, grave or intermediate pitch. Detailed discussion of
these differences belongs to the study of verse-forms.

(ii) A *syllable* is a non-signifying composite vocalization, comprising a
mute and a phoneme which has audible sound (thus *gr* is a syllable
without an *a*, and also with an *a*, i.e. *gra*). Detailed discussion of the
differences between syllables also belongs to the study of verse-
forms.

(iii) A *connective*[92] is:
57a  (a) A non-signifying vocalization which neither prevents nor

effects the composition of a single significant vocalization from two or more vocalizations, and which should not occur at the beginning of an utterance by itself (e.g. *men*, *dê*, *toi*, *de*). Or:

(b) A non-signifying vocalization which is capable of creating a single significant vocalization from two or more vocalizations which are themselves significant (e.g. 'around', 'about', etc.).

(iv) A *conjunction* is a non-signifying vocalization which marks the beginning, end or division of an utterance, and which may occur at the extremities as well as in the middle of an utterance.

(v) A *noun*[93] is a composite significant vocalization which does not express tense, no part of which is significant in its own right. (In nouns comprising two parts we do not treat either part as significant in its own right: e.g. the element -*dorus* in the name 'Theodorus' does not signify.)[94]

(vi) A *verb* is a composite significant vocalization which does express tense, no part of which is significant in its own right (just as with nouns). 'Person' or 'white' do not signify tense; the signification of 'walks' or 'walked' includes present and past tense respectively.

(vii) An *inflection* of a noun or verb is that which expresses (a) case ('of him', 'for him', etc.), (b) number (e.g. 'person', 'persons'), or (c) modes of expression, e.g. interrogative or imperative (thus 'did he walk?' and 'walk!' are inflections of the verb according to these two categories).

(viii) An *utterance* is a composite significant vocalization, part or parts of which are significant in their own right. Not every utterance is composed of a verb and a noun (e.g. the definition of 'human being'); it is possible for an utterance to contain no verb. But it will always contain a part which signifies something (e.g. 'Cleon' in 'Cleon walks'). An utterance may be single in two senses: either because it signifies a single object, or because it comprises a connected plurality of utterances (e.g. the *Iliad* is a single utterance by connection, the definition of 'human being' is a single utterance by virtue of signifying a single object).

## 9.3 *Classification of nouns*

21 Nouns are classed as simple (by which I mean those not compounded from significant parts, e.g. 'earth') or double. Double nouns may be composed of a significant and a non-signifying element (although within the noun itself there is no distinction between significant and non-signifying elements), or of two significant elements.[95] One may also have triple, quadruple or even multiplex nouns (e.g. most of those from Marseilles, such as 'Hermocaïcoxanthus').[96]

57b　　Nouns are classed as current, non-standard, metaphorical, ornamental, coined, lengthened, shortened and adapted.

By a *current* noun I mean one which is in use among a given people; by a *non-standard* noun I mean one which is in use among other people. Obviously the same noun may be both current and non-standard, but not for the same people. (*Sigunon* is current among the Cypriots, but non-standard to us; 'spear' is current among us, but non-standard to them.)

A *metaphor* is the application of a noun which properly applies to something else. The transfer may be from genus to species, from species to genus, from species to species, or by analogy:

(i) By a transfer from genus to species I mean (e.g.) 'Here stands my ship'; lying at anchor is one kind of standing.[97]

(ii) From species to genus: 'Odysseus has in truth performed ten thousand noble deeds'; ten thousand is a large number, and is used in place of 'many'.[98]

(iii) Species to species: e.g. 'drawing off the life with bronze' and 'cutting off water with edged bronze'; here 'drawing off' means cutting, and 'cutting' means drawing off – each is a kind of removal.[99]

(iv) By analogy I mean cases where B stands in a similar relation to A as D does to C; one can then mention D instead of B, and *vice versa*. Sometimes the thing to which the noun replaced stands in relation is expressed; I mean (e.g.) a cup stands in a similar relation to Dionysus as a shield does to Ares; so one may call a cup the 'shield of Dionysus', or a shield the 'cup of Ares'.[100] Or old age is to life as evening is to the day; so one may speak of evening as the old age of the day (as Empedocles does),[101] and of old age as the evening of life, or life's twilight. In some cases there is no existing noun for one term of the analogy, but it can nevertheless be expressed. For example scattering seed is 'sowing', but there is no noun for the scattering of fire from the sun; but this stands in a similar relation to the sun as sowing does to seed; hence the expression 'sowing the god-created fire'.[102] There is another way of using analogical metaphor: one may refer to something using the transferred noun, and negate some of its proper attributes; e.g. one might call a shield not 'the cup of Ares' but 'the wineless cup'.

An *ornamental* noun is . . .[103]

A *coined* noun is one that is not in use by anyone, but is posited by the poet himself. There seems to be a few nouns of this kind (e.g. 'sproutages' for horns and 'invocator' for priest).[104]

As for lengthening and shortening, a noun is *lengthened* if it has a 58a longer vowel than usual or an extra syllable; a noun is *shortened* if something has been removed. Examples of lengthening are *polêos* (for *poleôs*, 'of a city') and *Pêlêiadeô* (for *Pêleidou*, 'of Peleus' son'); of shortening, e.g. *kri* (for *krithê*, 'barley'), *dô* (for *dôma*, 'house') and 'from two eyes single *ops*' (for *opsis*, 'sight').[105]

An *adapted* noun is one in which part of the word is kept unchanged, and part added; e.g. 'by the rightward breast' (for 'right').[106]

Nouns themselves may be masculine, feminine or neuter. Masculine nouns are those ending in *n*, *r* and *s* (and its compounds, of which therè are two, *ps* and *ks*). Feminine nouns are those ending in those vowels which are invariably long, i.e. in *ê* and *ô*, and (among the vowels which are capable of being lengthened) in *a*.[107] (So the classes of masculine and feminine nouns turn out to be equal in number, since *ps* and *ks* are simply compound forms of *s*.) No noun ends in a mute or in a short vowel; only three end in *i* (i.e. *meli*, *kommi, peperi*), and five in *u* (i.e. *doru, pôu, napu, gonu, astu*). Neuters end in these and in *n, r* and *s*.

## 9.4 *Qualities of poetic style*

22  The most important quality in diction is clarity, provided there is no loss of dignity. The clearest diction is that based on current words; but that lacks dignity (as can be seen from the poetry of Cleophon, and that of Sthenelus).[108] By contrast, diction is distinguished and out of the ordinary when it makes use of exotic expressions – by which I mean non-standard words, metaphor, lengthening, and anything contrary to current usage. However, if one used nothing else the result would be a riddle or gibberish – a riddle if it were made up entirely of metaphors, gibberish if it were made up entirely of non-standard words. (The essence of a riddle is that it states facts by means of a combination of impossibilities; this cannot be done by putting other kinds of word together, but it is possible using metaphor; e.g. 'I saw a man welding bronze upon a man with fire',[109] and such like. And what is composed of non-standard words is gibberish.) So what is needed is some kind of mixture of these two things: one of them will make the diction out of the ordinary and avoid a loss of dignity (i.e. non-standard words, metaphor, ornament and the other categories I mentioned earlier), while current usage will contribute clarity.

58b  A major contribution to a style that is both clear and out of the ordinary is made by lengthenings, abbreviations and alterations. The variation from current usage makes the diction out of the ordinary, because we are not used to it; but it has something in common with what we are used to, so it will be clear. The people who find fault with this kind of style and satirize Homer are therefore mistaken in their criticism; e.g. the elder Eucleides argued that writing poetry is easy if one is allowed to use lengthening as much as one likes, and composed lampoons in the style in question: 'I saw Epichares walk-

ing to Marathon' and 'not mixing his hellebore'.[110] Admittedly, ob-
trusive use of this style is absurd; but moderation is equally necessary
in all aspects of diction; using metaphors, non-standard words and
the other categories in an inappropriate and deliberately absurd way
would produce the same effect. The difference that appropriateness
makes in the case of epic poetry can be observed if one inserts the
ordinary words into the verse. Equally in the case of non-standard
words, metaphors and the other kinds, the truth of what I am saying
is obvious if one substitutes current words. For example, Aeschylus
and Euripides composed identical lines of iambic verse; but the
change of a single word – a non-standard word in place of a current
one – made one line seem excellent, and the other trivial by comparison. Aeschylus wrote, in his *Philoctetes*, 'the canker that eats up
my foot's flesh'; Euripides substituted 'feasts on' for 'eats up'.[111] Also
in 'a scant and strengthless and unseemly man' one could substitute
current words: 'a little, weak, ugly man'. And in 'setting down an un-
comely chair and scant table': 'setting down a second-rate chair and
little table'. And in 'the sounding sea-shore': 'the shouting sea-
shore'.[112] Ariphrades, too, ridiculed the tragedians for using expressions that nobody would use in conversation, e.g. 'the house without' (for 'outside the house'), 'of thine', 'Achilles round about' (for   59a
'around Achilles'), etc. Things of this sort all make diction out of the
ordinary because they are not part of current usage. Ariphrades
failed to understand this.[113]

  It is important to use all the things I have mentioned appropri-
ately, including compound and non-standard words; but the most important thing is to be good at using metaphor. This is the one thing
that cannot be learnt from someone else, and is a sign of natural
talent; for the successful use of metaphor is a matter of perceiving
similarities. Compound words are most appropriate in dithyramb,
non-standard words in heroic verse, and metaphor in iambics. In
heroic verse all the things I have mentioned have their use; but in
iambic verse, because of its close resemblance to ordinary speech,[114]
the most appropriate words are the ones which could also be used in

prose speeches – i.e. current words, metaphor and ornamental words.

# 10. EPIC

## 10.1 *Plot*

23 Tragedy and imitation in action has been adequately covered in what has already been said. As for the art of imitation in narrative verse, it is clear that the plots ought (as in tragedy) to be constructed dramatically; that is, they should be concerned with a unified action, whole and complete, possessing a beginning, middle parts and an end, so that (like a living organism) the unified whole can effect its characteristic pleasure. They should not be organized in the same way as histories, in which one has to describe not a single action, but a single period of time, i.e. all the events that occurred during that period involving one or more people, each of which has an arbitrary relation to the others. The naval engagement at Salamis and the battle against the Carthaginians in Sicily occurred simultaneously without in any way tending towards the same end;[115] in exactly the same way one thing may follow another in succession over a period of time without their producing a single result. But perhaps the majority of poets compose in this way.

So (as we have already said) Homer's brilliance is evident in this respect as well, in comparison with other poets. He did not even try to treat the war as a whole, although it does have a beginning and an end. Had he done so, the plot would have been excessively large and difficult to take in at one view – or, if it had been moderate in magnitude, it would have been over-complicated in its variety. Instead, he has taken one part and used many others as episodes (e.g. the catalogue of ships,[116] and other episodes which he uses to diversify his

composition). The other poets write about a single person, a single   59b
period of time, or a single action of many parts – e.g. the poet of the
*Cypria* and the *Little Iliad*.[117] This means that only one tragedy can
be made out of the *Iliad* and *Odyssey*, or at most two, but many out
of the *Cypria* and the *Little Iliad* (more than eight, e.g. *Adjudication of
Arms*, *Philoctetes*, *Neoptolemus*, *Eurypylus*, *Beggary*, *Spartan Women*,
*Sack of Troy*, *Putting to Sea*; also *Sinon* and *Trojan Women*).

## 10.2 *Kinds and parts of epic*

Epic must also have the same kinds as tragedy; it is either simple or   24
complex, or based on character or on suffering.[118] The component
parts, except for lyric poetry and spectacle, are also the same; it too
needs reversals, recognitions and sufferings, and the reasoning and
diction should be of high quality. Homer was the first to use all of
these elements in a completely satisfactory way. Each of his two
poems has a different structure; the *Iliad* is simple and based on suffering, the *Odyssey* is complex (recognition pervades it) and based
on character. In addition, he excels everyone in diction and
reasoning.

## 10.3 *Differences between tragedy and epic*

Epic is differentiated in the length of its plot-structure and in its
verse-form. The stated definition of length is adequate; one must be
able to take in the beginning and the end in one view. This would
be the case if the structures were shorter than those of the ancient
epics, and matched the number of tragedies presented at one sitting.[119] Epic has an important distinctive resource for extending its
length. In tragedy it is not possible to imitate many parts of the
action being carried on simultaneously, but only the one on stage
involving the actors. But in epic, because it is narrative, it is possible

to treat many parts being carried on simultaneously; and these (provided that they are germane) make the poem more impressive. So epic has this advantage in achieving grandeur, variety of interest for the hearer and diversity of episodes; similarity quickly palls, and may cause tragedies to fail.

As for the verse-form, experience has proved the appropriateness of the heroic verse. If one were to compose a narrative imitation in some other verse-form, or a combination of them, it would seem unsuitable. Heroic verse is the most stately and grandiose form of verse; this is why it is particularly receptive to non-standard words and metaphors (for narrative imitation departs further from the norm than other kinds). Iambic verse and the trochaic tetrameter express movement (the latter having a dance-like quality, and the former being suited to action). It would be still more peculiar if one mixed them, as Chaeremon did.[120] For this reason no one has composed a long structure in any verse-form other than the heroic; as we have said, nature itself teaches people to choose what is appropriate to it.

60a

## 10.4 *Quasi-dramatic epic*

Homer deserves praise for many reasons, but above all because he alone among poets is not ignorant of what he should do in his own person. The poet in person should say as little as possible; that is not what makes him an imitator. Other poets perform in person throughout, and imitate little and seldom; but after a brief preamble Homer introduces a man or woman or some other character – and none of them are characterless: they have character.

## 10.5 *Astonishment and irrationalities*

While it is true that astonishment is an effect which should be sought in tragedy, the irrational (which is the most important source of astonishment) is more feasible in epic, because one is not looking at the agent. The pursuit of Hector would seem preposterous on stage, with the others standing by and taking no part in the pursuit while Achilles shakes his head to restrain them; but in epic it escapes notice.[121] Astonishment gives pleasure; evidence of this is the fact that everyone exaggerates when passing on news, on the assumption that they are giving pleasure.

Homer, in particular, taught other poets the right way to tell falsehoods. This is the false inference. In cases where the existence or occurrence of $A$ implies the existence or occurrence of $B$, people imagine that if $B$ is the case then $A$ also exists or occurs – which is fallacious. So if $A$ is false, but its existence would entail the existence or occurrence of $B$, one should add $B$; then, on the basis of its knowledge that $B$ is true, our mind falsely infers the reality of $A$ as well. An example of this can be found in the bath-scene.[122]

Probable impossibilities are preferable to implausible possibilities. Stories should not be constructed from irrational parts; so far as possible they should contain nothing irrational – or, failing that, it should be outside the narration (like Oedipus' ignorance of the manner of Laius' death)[123] and not in the play itself (like the report of the Pythian Games in the *Electra*, or the man who comes from Tegea to Mysia without speaking in the *Mysians*).[124] Saying that the plot would have been ruined otherwise is absurd; plots should not be constructed like that in the first place. But if one does posit an irrationality and it seems more or less rational, even an oddity is possible;[125] the irrationalities involved in Odysseus' being put ashore in the *Odyssey* would be manifestly intolerable if a second-rate poet 60b had composed them, but as it is the poet conceals the absurdity with other good qualities, and makes it a source of pleasure.[126]

## 10.6 *Diction*

Diction should be handled with particular care in those parts in which little is happening, and which are expressive neither of character nor of reasoning; excessively brilliant diction overshadows character and reasoning.

# 11. PROBLEMS AND SOLUTIONS

## 11.1 *Principles*

25 As for problems and their solutions, their number and the classes into which they fall should become clear if considered in this way:

(i) The poet is engaged in imitation, just like a painter or anyone else who produces visual images, and the object of his imitation must in every case be one of three things: either the kind of thing that was or is the case; or the kind of thing that is said or thought to be the case; or the kind of thing that ought to be the case.

(ii) The diction in which these things are expressed includes non-standard words, metaphors and many modifications of diction; these licences are allowed to poets.

(iii) In addition, correctness is not the same thing in ethics and poetry, nor in any other art and poetry. Error in poetry is of two kinds, one intrinsic, the other incidental. If someone has chosen to imitate accurately but failed to do so because of incompetence, the fault is intrinsic; but if he has chosen not to do so correctly (e.g. to show a horse with both right legs thrown forward) the error is in respect to the particular art (e.g. in respect to medicine or some other art), not in respect to the art of poetry itself.[127]

## II.2 *Applications*

So one should solve the objections posed in problems by considering them on the basis of these principles.

(i) First, those with regard to the art of poetry itself. If impossibilities have been included in a poem, that is an error; but it is correct if it attains the end of the art itself (the end has been stated above): i.e. if it makes either this or some other part have greater impact. An example is the pursuit of Hector.[128] If, however, it is possible for the end to be achieved as well or better without contravening the art concerned with those matters, then the error is not correct; there should if possible be no error at all.

(ii) Also, which class does the error belong to: those in respect of the art, or those in respect of some other incidental? It is less serious if the artist was unaware of the fact that a female deer does not have antlers than if he painted a poor imitation.

(iii) Furthermore, if the objection is that something is not true, perhaps it is as it ought to be; e.g. Sophocles said that he portrayed people as they should be, Euripides as they are. That is the solution to use.

(iv) If it is neither true nor as it ought to be, one might reply that this is what people say; e.g. stories about the gods: it may be that talking like that is neither an idealization nor the truth, and perhaps Xenophanes was right;[129] but at any rate, that is what 61a people say.

(v) Other things, though not idealizations, may perhaps reflect the way things used to be; e.g. the passage about the weapons, 'their spears stood upright on the butt-end' – that was the norm then (as it is even now among the Illyrians).[130]

(vi) In evaluating any utterance or action, one must take into account not just the moral qualities of what is actually done or said, but also the identity of the agent or speaker, the addressee, the occasion, the means, and the motive (e.g. whether it is to bring about a greater good or avert a greater evil).

(vii) Other problems should be solved with an eye to diction. For example a non-standard word may provide the solution to 'first the mules' (perhaps he does not mean mules but sentinels),[131] Dolon being 'ugly in appearance' (not physically deformed but facially disfigured, since Cretans call facial beauty 'beauty of appearance'),[132] and 'mix the wine stronger' (not undiluted, as for drunkards, but faster).[133] Other things are said metaphorically, e.g. 'all the gods and men slept through the night', while at the same time he says 'when he looked out over the Trojan plain . . . the sound of pipes and pan-pipes'; 'all' is said metaphorically for 'many', since all is a lot.[134] Also 'alone with no share' is metaphorical, the best known instance being unique.[135]

(viii) With reference to pronunciation, as in Hippias of Thasos' solution to 'we grant him achievement of glory' and 'part is rotted by rain'.[136]

(ix) Punctuation provides the solution to some problems; e.g. Empedocles: 'at once mortal things were born that before were immortal, and things unmixed formerly mixed'.[137]

(x) So does ambiguity; e.g. 'more of the night has passed' – 'more' is ambiguous.[138]

(xi) Other problems can be solved with reference to linguistic usage. We call diluted wine 'wine'; hence the phrase 'greaves of new-forged tin'. We call people who work iron 'bronze-smiths'; hence Ganymede is said to pour wine for Zeus, although the gods do not drink wine (this could also be metaphorical).[139]

(xii) Whenever a word seems to imply a contradiction, one should consider the number of meanings it could bear in the context; e.g. in 'by it was the bronze spear stayed' – how many different possible ways are there for it to be stopped there, in one way or another, however one might best take it?[140] (This is the exact *61b* opposite of what Glaucon describes,[141] when he says that some people make unreasonable prior assumptions and then, although

44

the adverse verdict is one they have reached by themselves, they make inferences from it and if anything contradicts their own ideas they criticize the poet as if *he* had expressed *their* opinion. This is what has occurred in the case of Icarius.[142] People assume that he is a Spartan, and that Telemachus' not meeting him when he went to Sparta is therefore odd. But perhaps the Cephallenians are right when they say that Odysseus married from among them, and that his name is Icadius not Icarius. So probably the problem is based on a misconception.)

## 11.3 *Conclusion*

In general:

(i) Impossibilities should be referred to poetic effect, or idealization of the truth, or opinion. With regard to poetic effect, a plausible impossibility is preferable to what is implausible but possible. Again, it is impossible for people to be as Zeuxis painted them, but that is an idealization of the truth; one should surpass the model.[143]

(ii) Irrationalities should be referred to what people say: that is one solution, and also sometimes that it is not irrational, since it is probable that improbable things will happen.[144]

(iii) Contradictory utterances should be subjected to the same scrutiny as refutations in arguments (i.e. is the same thing said, with reference to the same thing, and in the same sense?), to establish whether the poet contradicts either what he says himself or what a reasonable person would assume.[145]

(iv) An objection, either to irrationality or to depravity, is correct when there is no necessity and the poet makes no use of the irrationality (as Euripides fails to use Aegeus) or of the wickedness (as that of Menelaus in the *Orestes*).[146]

So the objections people make are of five kinds, i.e. that

something is impossible, irrational, harmful, contradictory, or contrary to correctness in the art. Solutions should be sought from those enumerated; there are twelve of them.[147]


# 12. COMPARATIVE EVALUATION OF EPIC AND TRAGEDY

26  One might pose the question whether epic imitation or tragic is superior.


## 12.1 *The case against tragedy*

If the less vulgar art is superior, and in all cases what is addressed to a superior audience is less vulgar, then it is perfectly clear that the art which imitates indiscriminately is vulgar. Assuming that the audience is incapable of grasping what the performer does not supply in person, they engage in a great deal of movement (as second-rate pipers spin round if they have to imitate throwing a discus, and drag the chorus-leader about if they have to play the *Scylla*).[148] Tragedy is like that. This is in fact the opinion which older actors held about those who came after them; Mynniscus used to call Callippides

62a  'monkey' because of his excesses, and Pindarus was viewed in much the same way.[149] The whole art of tragedy stands in the same relation to epic as these do to the others. So it is argued that epic is addressed to decent audiences who do not need gestures, while tragedy is addressed to second-rate audiences; if, then, tragedy is vulgar, clearly it must be inferior.

## 12.2 *Reply*

(i) First of all, this is not a criticism of the art of poetry but of the art of performance. A rhapsode performing epic poetry can make exaggerated use of gestures (like Sosistratus; so can a singer (this is what Mnasitheus of Opus used to do).[150]

(ii) Next, not all movement is to be disparaged (any more than all dance is), but only that of inferior persons. This is the objection that used to be made against Callippides, and is made now against others, on the grounds that the women they imitate are not respectable.[151]

(iii) Also, tragedy has its effect without movement, just as epic does: its quality is clear from reading.

So if tragedy is superior in other respects, this criticism at any rate does not necessarily apply to it. Further:

(iv) Tragedy has everything that epic does (it can even make use of its verse-form), and additionally it has as a major component part music and spectacle; this is a source of intense pleasure.

(v) Also it has vividness in reading as well as in performance.

(vi) Also, the end of imitation is attained in shorter length; what is more concentrated is more pleasant than what is watered down by being extended in time (I mean, for example, if one were to turn Sophocles' *Oedipus* into as many lines as the *Iliad* has). *62b*

(vii) Also the epic poets' imitation is less unified (an indication of this is that more than one tragedy comes from any given imitation). So if they treat a unified plot, either the exposition is brief and appears curtailed, or else it adheres to the length of that verse-form and is diluted.[152] (I mean, for example, if it comprises a number of actions. The *Iliad* and *Odyssey* have many parts of this kind, which possess magnitude in their own right; and yet the construction of these poems could not be improved upon, and they are an imitation of a single action to the greatest possible degree.)

47

So tragedy surpasses epic in all these respects, and also in artistic effect (since they should not produce any arbitrary pleasure but the one specified); clearly, then, because it achieves its purpose more effectively than epic, tragedy must be superior.

# 13. CONCLUSION

So much for tragedy and epic, the number and variety of their forms and component parts, the causes of their success and failure, and criticisms and solutions.

# NOTES TO THE
# TRANSLATION

**1.** For 'imitation' (*mimêsis*) see Introduction §2. The dithyramb was a kind of lyric poetry performed by a chorus. Pipe (*aulos*) and lyre (*kithara*) were the two most common forms of Greek wind and string instrument; the addition of the pan-pipes (*syrinx*) below implies a more general concept of instrumental music.

**2.** The reference is to the mimicry of, for example, animal noises (cf. Plato, *Republic*, 397a, *Laws*, 669c–d).

**3.** Sophron and his son Xenarchus worked in Syracuse in the late fifth century; their sketches of everyday life, and the philosophical dialogues of Plato and Xenophon (and others whose works have not survived), are cited as examples of imitation in prose.

**4.** The fifth-century philosopher Empedocles expounded his theories of nature in hexameter verse. Aristotle greatly admired the artistic quality of his work: fragment 70 (from *On Poets*) comments on his 'Homeric' mastery of poetic language, and especially his use of metaphor; he is cited several times in the *Poetics* (57b13f., 24, 58a5, 61a24f.). The present point is therefore not evaluative, but intended to define a restricted technical usage for the term 'poetry'.

**5.** A fourth-century tragic poet; little is known about his *Centaur* (see also 60a2), apparently a piece for recitation ('rhapsody') in a variety of metres.

**6.** The nome, like the dithyramb (n.1), was a kind of choral lyric.

**7.** All fifth-century painters. Polygnotus (cf. 50a27f. and n. 25) is famous; little is known of the other two, but at *Politics*, 1340a35–8 Pauson's work is described as less suitable for young people to view than that of Polygnotus.

**8.** Cleophon may be the fourth-century tragic poet of that name; on his style cf. 58a18–21. Hegemon wrote epic burlesques in the late fifth century; Nicochares' *Deiliad* (derived from *deilos*, 'cowardly', by analogy with *Iliad*) also suggests epic burlesque.

**9.** For dithyramb and nome cf. 47b26 (n. 6). Timotheus (cf. 54a30f. and n. 61) was a lyric poet of the late fifth and early fourth centuries noted for musical and stylistic innovations; his poem is presumably mentioned as an example of a serious treatment of the Cyclops Polyphemus, since the portrayal of Polyphemus by Philoxenus of Cythera was said to be a caricature of the tyrant Dionysius I, whose mistress the poet had seduced. But the text here is uncertain, and we cannot be quite sure what point Aristotle is making.

10. For Homer's quasi-dramatic style, making extensive use of direct speech, cf. 48b34–8, 60a5–11. Aristotle's classification of modes is an adaptation of Plato's (*Republic*, 392d–4c); unlike Aristotle, Plato regarded the dramatic mode with disfavour.

11. The verb for 'do' here is *dran*, whence 'drama'. The Dorian claim to have invented tragedy and comedy assumes (as becomes clear at the end of the following digression) that *dran* implies an origin among speakers of the Doric dialect; Aristotle is rightly sceptical of this assumption, and of the alleged derivation of 'comedy' from *kômê* ('village'). The democracy of the city of Megara in mainland Greece is dated to the sixth century BC; the Megarians in Sicily are the colonists at Megara Hyblaea. Epicharmus (from another Sicilian city, Syracuse) worked in the late sixth and early fifth centuries, not really 'much earlier' than the Athenian comic poets Chionides and Magnes (active from the 480s and 470s).

12. The 'two causes' are probably the human instincts for (a) imitation and (b) melody and rhythm (48b20f.). Many interpreters try to identify two distinct causes related to imitation; but this would not explain poetry as imitation *in verse*. The human instinct for rhythm and melody is also recognized by Plato (*Laws*, 653d–654a).

13. A rhythm can in principle be continued indefinitely; a verse-form such as the dactylic hexameter is a defined segment of that potentially infinite rhythmic continuum. Cf. *Rhetoric*, 1408b29.

14. That is, one imitating inferior agents. The *Margites* was not an invective, but a burlesque narrative about a hero of wide-ranging incompetence (he 'knew many things, but knew them all badly'). The attribution of the poem to Homer makes it antedate the earliest extant lampoons (those of the seventh-century poet Archilochus); but Aristotle reasonably infers that there must have been earlier lampoonists whose poems had not been preserved.

15. For Homer's quasi-dramatic style cf. 48a21f. (n. 10), 60a5–11.

16. The assumption is that a chorus-leader singing a solo response to the choral parts was the first step towards an actor wholly separate from the chorus. The number of actors was subsequently increased to two and three

(49a16–19); but it remained the custom in Greek theatre for a limited number of actors to play all the roles.

**17**. Satyr-plays were mythological burlesques with a chorus of satyrs (idle, drunken and lascivious followers of Dionysus, with a mixture of human and animal features), written and produced by tragic dramatists as a regular part of the tragic competition. Aristotle infers that they preserve characteristics of tragedy's pre-dramatic choral antecedents (cf. 49a10–13 and n. 16) which had disappeared in the evolution of tragedy proper. The text of this whole sentence is extremely uncertain.

**18**. On the characteristics of iambic verse cf. 59a10–13, 59b34–8, *Rhetoric*, 1404a29–33.

**19**. By contrast tragedy evokes fear and pity, emotions which Aristotle defines as responses to painful and destructive harm (*Rhetoric*, 1382a21f., 1385b13f.; cf. 52b11f. below). A mask like that of the blinded Oedipus, distorted by agonizing wounds, fulfils the function of tragedy, but would be out of place in comedy.

**20**. The archon chose the poets to compete in an Athenian dramatic festival, and assigned a wealthy citizen to each to finance the production-costs (especially the costume and training of the chorus). The earliest official comic competition in Athens was in 486 BC.

**21**. By 'universalized' Aristotle means constructed in accordance with necessity or probability; cf. chapter 9 below. Crates was an Athenian comic dramatist active from *c.* 450 BC.

**22**. By imitation in hexameter verse Aristotle means epic; his discussion begins in chapter 23. The promised discussion of comedy is not included in the extant *Poetics*; it was probably contained in a lost second book.

**23**. *Katharsis*: see Introduction §8.

**24**. The text and interpretation of this sentence are extremely uncertain.

**25**. For Polygnotus cf. 48a5f. (n. 7); he is cited as an example of painters good at portraying character at *Politics*, 1340a37f. Zeuxis, a painter active in the late fifth and early fourth centuries, reappears at 61b12f. to illustrate idealization in portraiture.

**26**. For reversals and recognitions see chapter 11.

**27**. Statesmanship forms judgements on the right conduct of public affairs; statesmen may express these judgements using natural eloquence, or exploiting the systematized persuasive techniques of rhetoric. Speech expressive of character and moral choice (*prohairesis*) is contrasted with speech based on reasoning at *Rhetoric*, 1417a16–28.

**28**. Litigants in the Athenian courts were allocated a limited time for their speeches, measured by a water-clock. But the last part of this sentence has never been satisfactorily explained.

**29**. As a young man Odysseus was wounded by a boar during a hunt; later he tried to avoid joining the Greek expedition against Troy by pretending to be insane. There is no causal relationship between these two events. The wounding is, in fact, recounted in *Odyssey*, 19.393–466, to explain the scar which establishes Odysseus' identity (see 54b26–30 and n. 71); but it is not part of the poem's plot, which is Aristotle's current concern.

**30**. For Aristotle's view of history cf. 59a21–9.

**31**. Agathon was a prominent Athenian tragic poet of the late fifth century (Plato's *Symposium* is set at a party celebrating his first victory, in 416 BC); cf. 56a18f., 24f., 29f. His *Antheus* is otherwise unknown.

**32**. The same word (*poiêtês*) means both 'poet' and 'maker'. Aristotle's point (here as in chapter 1) is that writing in verse is not sufficient to identify a poet; the poet is an imitator of action, and therefore a maker of plots.

**33**. 'Simple' is defined in chapter 10.

**34**. Greek dramatic festivals were competitive events, and there had been a competition between the leading actors (separate from that between the dramatists) since 449 BC. Aristotle comments on the contemporary dominance of actors over poets at *Rhetoric*, 1403b33.

**35**. An Argive named Mitys is mentioned in a speech falsely attributed to Demosthenes (59.33); nothing more is known about the incident referred to here.

**36**. At Sophocles, *Oedipus*, 924ff. a messenger brings the good (934) news that Oedipus has succeeded to the Corinthian throne on the death of his supposed father; when he learns that Oedipus is reluctant to return to Corinth for fear of committing incest with his mother, he is eager to allay that fear too (1002ff.); but in doing so he sets in train the sequence of events which leads to the discovery of Oedipus' parricide and incest.

**37**. For the *Lynceus*, by Aristotle's friend Theodectes, see 55b29–32 (n. 82).

**38**. *Philia*: see Introduction, §7. As Aristotle goes on to say, this is not the only kind of recognition; but its close bearing on good and bad fortune makes it particularly effective in tragedy.

**39**. For the recognitions in Euripides' *Iphigeneia in Tauris* see 54a7, 54b31–6 (n. 72), 55a18f., 55b3–12.

**40**. For this section see Introduction, n.10.

**41**. *Hamartia*: see Introduction §7.

**42.** Referring to the *outcome*; this does not contradict the statement that the *structure* of the plot should be complex rather than (in a different sense) simple (52a12–18, 52b31f.).

**43.** Alcmeon, like Orestes, avenged his father's death by killing his mother (cf. 53b24f., 33); Oedipus killed his father and slept with his mother in ignorance of their identity; likewise Meleager and Telephus killed their uncles; Thyestes unwittingly ate his children's flesh (served to him at a feast by his brother Atreus in revenge for the seduction of the latter's wife) and committed incest with his own daughter.

**44.** That is, Euripides' critics make the same mistake as the advocates of the double outcome mentioned in the previous paragraph.

**45.** Odysseus triumphs, the wicked suitors are killed (cf. 55b22f.).

**46.** In tragedy Orestes kills Aegisthus to avenge his father's death. The fourth-century comic poet Alexis wrote an *Orestes*, but we do not know whether Aristotle is alluding to the plot of that (or some similar) play or suggesting a hypothetical extreme.

**47.** *Philoi*: cf. n. 38 and Introduction §7.

**48.** Both cases of matricide (cf. n. 43).

**49.** In Euripides' *Medea*, Medea punishes the infidelity of her husband Jason by killing their children.

**50.** Astydamas was a leading tragic dramatist in the mid fourth century; it is not known how he contrived to keep Alcmeon (cf. 53a20 and n. 43, 53b24) in ignorance of his mother's identity. In *Odysseus Wounded*, a lost play by Sophocles, Telegonus was Odysseus' son by Circe; having never seen his father, he did not recognize him when they fought.

**51.** One possibility (knowing and not acting) has been overlooked in the foregoing enumeration, although it is included (somewhat dismissively) in the following ranking. It does appear in the Arabic translation (after the reference to Medea at 53b29); but 'third possibility' at 53b34 suggests that this may be a later addition by a reader who has noticed the omission.

**52.** Sophocles, *Antigone*, 1231–7: the distraught Haemon tries to stab his father Creon, and then in remorse kills himself.

**53.** The *Cresphontes* is a lost play by Euripides. When Merope's husband was murdered she managed to smuggle their baby son Cresphontes to safety; many years later she tries to kill the stranger who comes to claim the reward for killing Cresphontes, but discovers before it is too late that the stranger is Cresphontes himself, returning in disguise to avenge his father's death.

**54.** See the summary of the story at 55b3–12.

**55**. Nothing is known of this play; and while Helle's family (including Athamas, Phrixus and Ino) was fertile in tragic events, none of the attested stories corresponds to the incident Aristotle describes here.

**56**. In chapter 13 (53a18–22).

**57**. For Aristotle's views on whether and in what sense slaves and women can be 'good' cf. especially *Politics*, 1.13 (1259b18–60b24).

**58**. The character should display the right kind of goodness; a good woman should be courageous, but not in the same way as a man (cf. *Politics*, 1260a20–24, 1277b20–25; 'a man would be regarded as a coward if he were courageous in the same way that a woman is courageous'). 'Cleverness' looks forward to the example of Melanippe below (54a31 and n. 62).

**59**. The reference is obscure; Aristotle probably means 'like us' (the pre-condition of fear at 53a4–6, and cf. 48a4–14). See Introduction §9.

**60**. In Euripides' *Orestes* Menelaus' failure to support his nephew Orestes violates the obligations owed to a *philos* (see Introduction §7); the example recurs at 61b21.

**61**. A dithyramb (also mentioned at 61b32) by Timotheus (48a15 and n. 9) which portrayed Odysseus lamenting the loss of his comrades, eaten by the monster Scylla (cf. *Odyssey*, 12.234–59).

**62**. The reference is to Euripides' lost *Melanippe the Wise*. Melanippe gave birth to twins by the god Poseidon, and exposed them; when the babies were found being suckled by a cow Melanippe's father, assuming that the cow had given birth to them, decided to have them destroyed as unnatural monsters. Melanippe tried to prevent this by arguing that the cow could not have given birth to human children; her speech included advanced cosmo-logical and theological arguments, thus displaying a cleverness inappropriate in a woman (cf. n. 58).

**63**. In Euripides' *Iphigeneia in Aulis* Iphigeneia's first reaction on learning that she is to be sacrificed to Artemis to secure the Greek army's passage to Troy is to plead for her life (1211–52); but later she patriotically embraces her fate (1368–1401).

**64**. 'Resolution' is defined in chapter 18 (55b24–32); cf. 56a9f. for poor technique in resolutions. 'Theatrical device' renders *mêkhanê*; literally, this was a crane used in the Greek theatre for the appearance of a god who might conclude the play by outlining subsequent events or (less appropri-ately, in Aristotle's view) by imposing an arbitrary resolution on the plot. The two examples are Euripides' *Medea*, in which Medea's escape from Corinth after the killing of her children (see 53b29 and n. 49) is contrived by means of a supernatural chariot, and *Iliad*, 2.109–210, where Agamemnon proposes abandoning the siege of Troy in an oblique attempt to stimulate the army's fighting spirit; but the army, taking the proposal at face value, accepts it with enthusiasm, and the goddess Athene has to intervene to resolve the crisis which ensues.

**65.** Referring to Oedipus' ignorance of the circumstances of Laius' death (see 60a30).

**66.** The text of this sentence is uncertain.

**67.** No one knows what this paragraph means. By 'published works' Aristotle presumably means his *On Poets*.

**68.** The 'earth-born' were the men who sprang from the dragon's teeth sown by Cadmus; their descendants had a birth-mark in the shape of a spearhead. In one version of the story, Creon recognized Maeon, son of Haemon and Antigone, by this mark; but we do not know the source of the line which Aristotle quotes.

**69.** Carcinus was a tragic poet of the early fourth century (cf. 55a26–9). We do not know anything about the plot of this play; for Thyestes see 53a21 (n. 43); the star-shaped birthmark was a characteristic of his family (the descendants of Pelops).

**70.** Tyro set her twin sons by Poseidon adrift in a small boat; in Sophocles' (lost) *Tyro* the boat served as a recognition-token.

**71.** In the bath-scene (*Odyssey*, 19.386–475; cf. 60a25f. and n.122) the Nurse penetrates Odysseus' disguise when she observes his scar (cf. 51a26 and n. 29). This is an unplanned consequence of Odysseus' own request (19.343–8) that his feet be washed by one of the older female servants, and is thus linked to a reversal. But in *Odyssey*, 21.188–224 Odysseus simply declares his identity to the herdsmen Eumaeus and Philoetius, and shows them the scar by way of confirmation.

**72.** In Euripides' *Iphigeneia in Tauris* (see 52b6–8 and n. 39) Iphigeneia's identity is revealed when she asks one of the two strangers to deliver a message addressed to her brother Orestes (769–94); Orestes then declares himself, confirming his identity by displaying knowledge of their home (808–26). Aristotle's point is that he could equally well have brought some physical recognition-token with him.

**73.** Tereus was married to Procne, and raped her sister Philomela. To keep his crime secret he cut out her tongue, but she wove a tapestry showing what had happened; this picture was the 'voice of the shuttle'.

**74.** Dicaeogenes was a late fifth-century tragedian; nothing is known of his

*Cyprians*. In *Odyssey*, 8.485–586 Odysseus weeps on hearing a song about the fall of Troy; this prompts his host Alcinous to enquire about his identity, and Odysseus's reply (*Odyssey*, 9–12) is the tale told to Alcinous.

**75**. In Aeschylus' *Choephori*, 166–211 Electra finds a lock of hair and a footprint at her father's tomb, and infers Orestes' presence from their similarity to her own. Despite this example, Aristotle is not thinking primarily of recognition through reasoning from signs, but (as the following examples make clearer) situations in which one character's reasoning discloses his or her identity to another. As with recognition through memory, a character's spontaneous response to the situation provides a clue by means of which their identity can be inferred.

**76**. Nothing more is known of Polyidus; his suggestion is mentioned again at 55b10f. For Theodectes cf. 52a27–9 (n. 37), 55b29–32 (n. 82); nothing more is known about his *Tydeus*. The *Sons of Phineus* is also unknown.

**77**. Unknown. Aristotle's account is very cryptic. Presumably Odysseus on his homecoming concealed his identity by bringing a false report of his own death; the audience is led to expect him to establish his identity by stringing the bow (which no one but Odysseus could do), but instead he is accepted simply because he recognizes the bow (which anyone who had seen or heard a report of it might do). For the exploitation of false inference by poets see also 60a18–26.

**78**. For Carcinus cf. n. 69; we have no further information about the mistake referred to here.

**79**. To imitate convincingly the poet must be able to project himself into the emotions of the subjects. This is made easier by the versatility of a genius or by the madman's weak grasp on his own identity; more generally, acting out the part with gestures may help. This was evidently a well-established view of a poet's method of work; Aristophanes has fun with it (*Thesmophoriazusae*, 156–8).

**80**. The universal here seems to be more abstract than in chapter 9. There universality rested on the necessary or probable connection between events; here it designates the barest outline of a story, which only becomes a plot with causally connected events when the outline is turned into episodes. The text of this parenthesis is uncertain.

**81**. Cf. 55a6–8 (n. 76).

**82**. Danaus ordered his daughters to kill their husbands; Hypermestra alone disobeyed, sparing her husband Lynceus; she bore his son, presumably keeping him and the child secret. In Theodectes' play the child must have been found and his parentage revealed; Danaus condemned Lynceus to death but somehow (cf. 52a27–9 and n. 37) this led to a reversal, and it was Danaus who died; Lynceus survived. But the text here is uncertain, and our limited knowledge of the play's plot makes it impossible to reconstruct Aristotle's words with complete confidence.

**83.** A perplexing statement: there has been no mention of *four* parts of tragedy before now. To add to the confusion, the name of the fourth kind has been lost in the Greek text; the conjectural text translated here makes the passage consistent with the cross-reference at 59b7–9 (another widely accepted conjecture makes the fourth kind the 'tragedy of spectacle'). The examples do little to cast light on Aristotle's meaning.

**84.** The obscurity of the preceding paragraph casts a shadow over this one as well. Presumably poets with a special talent for the depiction of character were criticized for failing to depict suffering as effectively as poets who specialized in that kind of tragedy, and *vice versa*.

**85.** For faulty resolutions cf. 54a37–b2.

**86.** The *Sack of Troy* was the title of an epic poem and of several lost tragedies; Euripides' *Trojan Women* and *Hecuba* both deal with events drawn from this larger story. The reference to *Niobe* is perplexing, since there was no epic on that subject; Aristotle perhaps wrote something different, but the text cannot be corrected with any confidence. We do not know what failure of Agathon (cf. n. 31) Aristotle is referring to.

**87.** The text and interpretation here are uncertain.

**88.** For Agathon cf. n. 31; and cf.61b15 for the principle stated here.

**89.** Instead of composing choral lyrics in the traditional way, the poet could simply mark the points at which the chorus should perform and leave it to the producer to choose the songs to be sung in these interludes. In comedy we can observe this being done sporadically by Aristophanes in his later work at the beginning of the fourth century, and consistently by Menander at the end of the fourth century.

**90.** *Iliad*, 1.1 Protagoras of Abdera was a leading fifth-century sophist.

**91.** The difference is that animal noises cannot be compounded into syllables.

**92.** The text is in a hopeless muddle here, and Aristotle's definitions of connective and conjunction cannot be restored with any confidence. The reconstruction adopted here counts as 'connectives' (a) the particles, much used in Greek, which convey a nuance (e.g. adding emphasis, or highlighting an antithesis) without changing the structure of the utterance, and (b) prepositions which link significant words together ('stab *in* the dark'), and possibly also co-ordinating conjunctions ('fog *and* confusion'); Aristotle's 'conjunctions' are then words which signal the articulation of complex utterances ('*since* the text is obscure, we can only guess', 'we must do *what* we can').

**93**. Aristotle's term applies to any signifying word which does not express tense, including adjectives and pronouns. But in the discussion of style in chapter 22, where verbs are also included, the term has reverted to its broader non-technical sense, 'word'.

**94**. The element -*dorus* derives from the word for 'gift'.

**95**. For example, 'outcome' contains a non-signifying element (the connective 'out': 57a6–10), while 'homecoming' comprises two significant elements; but in both cases it is the whole compound word which we treat as significant, not its separate components (cf. 57a12–14).

**96**. The Hermus, Caïcus and Xanthus are all rivers in the region of Phocaea, the city from which Marseilles was originally founded; the less extravagant compound Hermocaïcus is attested as a personal name at one of the colonies of Marseilles. The text here is uncertain.

**97**. *Oydssey*, 1.185.

**98**. *Iliad*, 2.272.

**99**. Empedocles fragments 138 and 143; the first quotation refers to a man being killed with a bronze weapon, the second to water being drawn off in a bronze bowl or bucket.

**100**. Timotheus fragment 21 Page (*PMG* 797).

**101**. Empedocles fragment 152; but the text here is uncertain, and we cannot be sure which phrase is being attributed to Empedocles.

**102**. Source unknown.

**103**. The discussion of ornamental nouns has dropped out of the Greek text; Aristotle has in mind the poetic use of epithets (as in '*rosy-fingered* dawn').

**104**. The source of 'sproutages' is unknown; 'invocator' (*arêtêr*) is Homeric.

**105**. All these examples are epic forms: *Pêlêiadeô* occurs in the first line of the *Iliad*. The quotation illustrating *ops* is Empedocles fragment 88.

**106**. *Iliad*, 5.393; Homer uses a comparative (*dexiteros*) in place of the standard *dexios*.

**107**. In Greek *ps* and *ks* are each written with a single letter. Different letters are used for the long and short forms of the vowels *e* and *o*; the other vowels have a single letter for both forms.

**108**. For Cleophon cf. 48a12 (n.8). Sthenelus was a tragic poet of the fifth century; his style was mocked by Aristophanes (fragment 158 Kassel-Austin).

**109**. This riddle describes a doctor applying a heated bronze cup to a wound to draw blood; the cup would be kept in place by suction as it cooled.

**110**. Eucleides is unknown. The two quotations grotesquely exaggerate a metrical freedom found in epic poetry. Epichares was an Athenian politician at the end of the fifth century; hellebore was used in the treatment of insanity.

**111**. Aeschylus fragment 253; Euripides fragment 792.

**112**. These three examples are from the *Odyssey* (9.515, 20.259) and *Iliad* (17.265).

**113**. Nothing is known of Ariphrades. I have omitted one more than normally untranslatable example from the foregoing list of poetic usages.

**114**. Cf. 49a24–8 (n. 18), 59b34–8.

**115**. The victories over the Persians at Salamis and over the Carthaginians at Himera in Sicily were said to have happened on the same day (Herodotus, *Histories* 7.166). For the contrast between poetry and history cf. chapter 9 (51a38–b7).

**116**. *Iliad*, 2.484–779; the catalogue relates to the beginning of the war rather than its tenth year, in which the *Iliad* is set.

**117**. The *Cypria* recounted the antecedents of the Trojan War; the *Little Iliad* took up the story from the end of the *Iliad*.

**118**. Cf. 55b32–56a3 and n. 83.

**119**. That is, three tragedies, amounting to 4,000–5,000 lines; by contrast, the *Iliad* is over 15,000 lines long and the *Odyssey* over 12,000.

**120**. Cf. 47b21f. (n. 5).

**121**. See *Iliad*, 22.131–207, cited again at 60b26. Cf. 55a22–9 for the care that dramatists have to take over what is seen on stage.

**122**. Cf. 54b26–30 (n. 71), and compare the discussion of false inference at 55a12–16. If the stranger is Odysseus, he will have a scar; but his having a scar does not (as the Nurse assumes) entail that he is Odysseus. Some think the reference is to the way the disguised Odysseus deceives Penelope just before the bath-scene (*Odyssey*, 19.213–60): if the stranger saw Odysseus, he will be able to describe him; but his ability to describe Odysseus does not entail that he saw him.

**123**. Cf. 54b7f.

**124**. Sophocles, *Electra*, 680–763 is a false report of Orestes' death in a chariot race at the Pythian games; the irrationality in question is an anachronism (since the Pythian games were founded much later). Aeschylus and Sophocles both wrote a play entitled *Mysians*, concerned with Telephus; because of the blood-guilt incurred by the killing of his uncle (53a21 and n. 43), he could speak to no one in the course of his lengthy journey.

**125.** The text and interpretation are uncertain.

**126.** In *Odyssey*, 13.116–25 the Phaeacians put the sleeping Odysseus ashore in Ithaca without his waking up. This implausible eventuality is contrived to enhance his homecoming (it makes possible the striking scene in which Odysseus is at first uncertain where he is, and then learns from Athene that he has arrived home); Homer distracts us from the implausibility by (for example) switching our attention to a discussion between Zeus and Poseidon.

**127.** The text in this paragraph is damaged, and Aristotle's argument cannot be reconstructed with complete certainty.

**128.** Cf. 60a14–17 (n. 121).

**129.** Xenophanes, a poet and philosopher active in the late sixth and early fifth centuries, was critical of anthropomorphic theology, and objected strongly to the immoralities of the gods as portrayed in poetry. Compare the arguments in Plato, *Republic*, 2 (377d–383c).

**130.** *Iliad*, 10.152f. The objection is to an unfamiliar way of keeping spears at the ready.

**131.** *Iliad*, 1.50. The objection is to the triviality of the god Apollo paying attention to animals when he inflicts a plague on the Greek army; Aristotle's solution turns on a similarity between Greek words for 'mule' (*oureus*) and 'sentinel' (*ouros*).

**132.** *Iliad*, 10.316. The objection arises because Homer also describes Dolon as 'fleet of foot'.

**133.** *Iliad*, 9.203. Greeks drank wine diluted; Achilles' instruction seems to turn a serious meeting into a drunken party.

**134.** Aristotle means to quote *Iliad*, 10.1f. (the wording of which is slightly different in our manuscripts of Homer). How can everyone have been asleep if Zeus heard music (*Iliad*, 10.11–13)?

**135.** *Iliad*, 18.489, *Odyssey*, 5.275. Taken literally, Homer states that the Bear is the only constellation which never sets ('alone with no share of the baths of Ocean'); this is false, but the Bear is the best-known of those constellations which never set.

**136.** Hippias is unknown (this is not the famous sophist, Hippias of Elis). In *Iliad*, 2.15 Hippias changes the accent to make 'we grant' into the imperative 'grant'; this avoids attributing a lie directly to Zeus. (In our manuscripts of Homer the phrase in question occurs at 21.297 but not at 2.15, where the reading is 'sorrow is in store for the Trojans'.) In *Iliad*, 23.328 a different reading of the letters gives 'not rotted' instead of 'rotted'.

**137**. Empedocles (see 47b18 and n. 4) fragment 35.14f. Were the things 'unmixed formerly' or 'formerly mixed'?

**138**. *Iliad*, 10.252; the line may mean the majority of the night, i.e two-thirds, or more than two-thirds – which in context creates a contradiction.

**139**. The examples are from *Iliad*, 21.592 (the 'tin' armour must be an alloy of tin, which can be called 'tin' in the same way that diluted wine is called 'wine') and *Iliad*, 20.234 (Ganymede poured nectar for the gods).

**140**. *Iliad*, 20.272. A spear penetrates two layers of bronze, and is stopped by a layer of gold; but the gold (being for display) would be the outer layer.

**141**. Glaucon is unknown. The text here is uncertain, and it may be wrong to connect Glaucon to what follows.

**142**. If it is assumed that Penelope's father Icarius was a Spartan, it is odd that his grandson Telemachus does not meet him when he visits Sparta in *Odyssey*, 4; but the *Odyssey* does not say that he was a Spartan.

**143**. For Zeuxis cf. 50a26–8 (n. 25). The text of this sentence is uncertain.

**144**. Compare the remark attributed to Agathon at 56a23–5 (n. 88).

**145**. For example, Aristotle says that the best kind of tragic plot is 'complex rather than simple' (52b31f.) and that it is 'simple' (53a12f.); but 'simple' refers in one case to the structure of the plot and in the other to its outcome (n.42), so there is no contradiction.

**146**. In Euripides' *Medea*, 663 Aegeus' arrival has no necessary or probable connection with what precedes it; it is a coincidence, contrived to furnish Medea with an offer of asylum. For Menelaus' wickedness cf. 54a28f. (n. 60).

**147**. At first sight there seem to be at least thirteen. The approach adopted above (treating non-standard words and metaphors as variants of a single solution based on the kinds of departure from current usage listed in chapter 21) is perhaps the least arbitrary of the many that have been proposed.

**148**. For Timotheus' *Scylla* cf. 54a30f. (n. 61).

**149**. Mynniscus performed in Aeschylus' later plays (in the 460s) and was still active in 422 BC, when he won the actors' competition; Callippides (mentioned again at 62a9–11; cf. Xenophon, *Symposium*, 3.11) won a prize in 418 BC. Nothing is known about Pindarus.

**150**. Sosistratus and Mnasitheus are unknown.

**151**. For Callippides cf. 61b34–6 (n. 149). The objection is that his style of acting robbed female roles of the restraint and self-control to be looked for in respectable women.

152. See 59b31–60a5 for the association between the dactylic hexameter and extended narration. A unified plot must subsume a lot of actions to achieve the length appropriate to heroic verse (cf. 56a10–19); even Homer's poetry, which is excellently constructed (59a30–37), is diluted as a result of this, so *a fortiori* other inferior epics will be open to the same criticism.

# READ MORE IN PENGUIN

In every corner of the world, on every subject under the sun, Penguin represents quality and variety – the very best in publishing today.

For complete information about books available from Penguin – including Puffins, Penguin Classics and Arkana – and how to order them, write to us at the appropriate address below. Please note that for copyright reasons the selection of books varies from country to country.

**In the United Kingdom**: Please write to *Dept. EP, Penguin Books Ltd, Bath Road, Harmondsworth, West Drayton, Middlesex UB7 0DA*

**In the United States**: Please write to *Consumer Services, Penguin Putnam Inc., 405 Murray Hill Parkway, East Rutherford, New Jersey 07073-2136.* VISA and MasterCard holders call 1-800-631-8571 to order Penguin titles

**In Canada**: Please write to *Penguin Books Canada Ltd, 10 Alcorn Avenue, Suite 300, Toronto, Ontario M4V 3B2*

**In Australia**: Please write to *Penguin Books Australia Ltd, 487 Maroondah Highway, Ringwood, Victoria 3134*

**In New Zealand**: Please write to *Penguin Books (NZ) Ltd, Private Bag 102902, North Shore Mail Centre, Auckland 10*

**In India**: Please write to *Penguin Books India Pvt Ltd, 11 Community Centre, Panchsheel Park, New Delhi 110017*

**In the Netherlands**: Please write to *Penguin Books Netherlands bv, Postbus 3507, NL-1001 AH Amsterdam*

**In Germany**: Please write to *Penguin Books Deutschland GmbH, Metzlerstrasse 26, 60594 Frankfurt am Main*

**In Spain**: Please write to *Penguin Books S. A., Bravo Murillo 19, 1°B, 28015 Madrid*

**In Italy**: Please write to *Penguin Italia s.r.l., Via Vittorio Emanuele 45/a, 20094 Corsico, Milano*

**In France**: Please write to *Penguin France, 12, Rue Prosper Ferradou, 31700 Blagnac*

**In Japan**: Please write to *Penguin Books Japan Ltd, Iidabashi KM-Bldg, 2-23-9 Koraku, Bunkyo-Ku, Tokyo 112-0004*

**In South Africa**: Please write to *Penguin Books South Africa (Pty) Ltd, P.O. Box 751093, Gardenview, 2047 Johannesburg*

# READ MORE IN PENGUIN

## A CHOICE OF CLASSICS

| | |
|---|---|
| Aeschylus | **The Oresteian Trilogy** |
| | **Prometheus Bound/The Suppliants/Seven against Thebes/The Persians** |
| Aesop | **The Complete Fables** |
| Ammianus Marcellinus | **The Later Roman Empire (AD 354–378)** |
| Apollonius of Rhodes | **The Voyage of Argo** |
| Apuleius | **The Golden Ass** |
| Aristophanes | **The Knights/Peace/The Birds/The Assemblywomen/Wealth** |
| | **Lysistrata/The Acharnians/The Clouds** |
| | **The Wasps/The Poet and the Women/ The Frogs** |
| Aristotle | **The Art of Rhetoric** |
| | **The Athenian Constitution** |
| | **Classic Literary Criticism** |
| | **De Anima** |
| | **The Metaphysics** |
| | **Ethics** |
| | **Poetics** |
| | **The Politics** |
| Arrian | **The Campaigns of Alexander** |
| Marcus Aurelius | **Meditations** |
| Boethius | **The Consolation of Philosophy** |
| Caesar | **The Civil War** |
| | **The Conquest of Gaul** |
| Cicero | **Murder Trials** |
| | **The Nature of the Gods** |
| | **On the Good Life** |
| | **On Government** |
| | **Selected Letters** |
| | **Selected Political Speeches** |
| | **Selected Works** |
| Euripides | **Alcestis/Iphigenia in Tauris/Hippolytus** |
| | **The Bacchae/Ion/The Women of Troy/ Helen** |
| | **Medea/Hecabe/Electra/Heracles** |
| | **Orestes and Other Plays** |

# READ MORE IN PENGUIN

## A CHOICE OF CLASSICS

| | |
|---|---|
| Hesiod/Theognis | **Theogony/Works and Days/Elegies** |
| Hippocrates | **Hippocratic Writings** |
| Homer | **The Iliad** |
| | **The Odyssey** |
| Horace | **Complete Odes and Epodes** |
| Horace/Persius | **Satires and Epistles** |
| Juvenal | **The Sixteen Satires** |
| Livy | **The Early History of Rome** |
| | **Rome and Italy** |
| | **Rome and the Mediterranean** |
| | **The War with Hannibal** |
| Lucretius | **On the Nature of the Universe** |
| Martial | **Epigrams** |
| | **Martial in English** |
| Ovid | **The Erotic Poems** |
| | **Heroides** |
| | **Metamorphoses** |
| | **The Poems of Exile** |
| Pausanias | **Guide to Greece (in two volumes)** |
| Petronius/Seneca | **The Satyricon/The Apocolocyntosis** |
| Pindar | **The Odes** |
| Plato | **Early Socratic Dialogues** |
| | **Gorgias** |
| | **The Last Days of Socrates (Euthyphro/ The Apology/Crito/Phaedo)** |
| | **The Laws** |
| | **Phaedrus and Letters VII and VIII** |
| | **Philebus** |
| | **Protagoras/Meno** |
| | **The Republic** |
| | **The Symposium** |
| | **Theaetetus** |
| | **Timaeus/Critias** |
| Plautus | **The Pot of Gold and Other Plays** |
| | **The Rope and Other Plays** |

# READ MORE IN PENGUIN

## A CHOICE OF CLASSICS

| | |
|---|---|
| Pliny | The Letters of the Younger Pliny |
| Pliny the Elder | Natural History |
| Plotinus | The Enneads |
| Plutarch | The Age of Alexander (Nine Greek Lives) |
| | Essays |
| | The Fall of the Roman Republic (Six Lives) |
| | The Makers of Rome (Nine Lives) |
| | Plutarch on Sparta |
| | The Rise and Fall of Athens (Nine Greek Lives) |
| Polybius | The Rise of the Roman Empire |
| Procopius | The Secret History |
| Propertius | The Poems |
| Quintus Curtius Rufus | The History of Alexander |
| Sallust | The Jugurthine War/The Conspiracy of Cataline |
| Seneca | Dialogues and Letters |
| | Four Tragedies/Octavia |
| | Letters from a Stoic |
| | Seneca in English |
| Sophocles | Electra/Women of Trachis/Philoctetes/Ajax |
| | The Theban Plays |
| Suetonius | The Twelve Caesars |
| Tacitus | The Agricola/The Germania |
| | The Annals of Imperial Rome |
| | The Histories |
| Terence | The Comedies (The Girl from Andros/The Self-Tormentor/The Eunuch/Phormio/The Mother-in-Law/The Brothers) |
| Thucydides | History of the Peloponnesian War |
| Virgil | The Aeneid |
| | The Eclogues |
| | The Georgics |
| Xenophon | Conversations of Socrates |
| | Hiero the Tyrant |
| | A History of My Times |
| | The Persian Expedition |